Japan's New Buddhism

Japan's New Buddhism

AN OBJECTIVE ACCOUNT OF SOKA GAKKAI

by Kiyoaki Murata

foreword by Daisaku Ikeda

A Weatherhill Book
WALKER/WEATHERHILL
New York & Tokyo

FIRST EDITION, 1969

Published by John Weatherhill, Inc.
of New York and Tokyo
with editorial offices at
7-6-13 Roppongi, Minato-ku Tokyo 106
Distributed in the Far East by
JOHN WEATHERHILL, INC.
and in the United States by
WALKER AND COMPANY
720 Fifth Avenue, New York, N.Y. 10019
Copyright © in Japan, 1969
by John Weatherhill, Inc.
Printed in Japan

LCC CARD NO. 74-83640

Contents

Illustrations

Foreword

The author is one of the few Japanese newspapermen who have closely observed the Sokagakkai over many years. Books written so far about our organization contain fragmentary comments and are, regrettably, shallow in viewpoint and prejudiced. The author of this book, however, seems to have endeavored to free himself from prejudices and preoccupations in order to understand the doctrines of Nichiren Shoshu and the true nature of the Sokagakkai.

Frankly, it is well-nigh impossible to comprehend the profound system of Buddhist philosophy. Perhaps one may say it is absolutely impossible for a person outside its realm to understand it fully. This is the reason why our predecessors, from ancient times, have devoted their entire lives to the practice and study of Buddhist philosophy.

The author's introduction and interpretation of the doctrine of Nichiren Shoshu, therefore, represent what he has been able to grasp so far. As such, I wish to regard them as tentative. By this I mean that the philosophy of Buddhism becomes more profound as one's understanding deepens. To those who read this book with the awareness of this principle, therefore, the volume will undoubtedly prove helpful in their pursuit of the truth and meaning of Buddhism.

As for the facts given in this book concerning the Sokagakkai, I can say with assurance that the book is more accurate than any other on the subject. Some of the bits of information the author has dug out in the course of his research are printed for the first time.

Interest in the Sokagakkai is rapidly mounting not only in Japan but throughout the world. It is unfortunate that those

who take such interest have had to depend on books characterized by prejudice and inaccuracy and hence have come to
entertain misconceptions about the Sokagakkai. If such people
were to grasp facts accurately and objectively, I am certain
they would realize that the Sokagakkai represents a true mass
movement, a great bloodless revolution without precedent in
history, that aims to establish a human society in which life
and humanity are respected.

I hope that this work by Mr. Kiyoaki Murata will play a role
in bringing correct understanding of the Sokagakkai to many
people and will help to create the tide of the times that will
lead to the establishment of the future society.

DAISAKU IKEDA

Preface

It was the growing importance of Soka Gakkai that led to my first direct contact with the organization back in July 1956 when I had the opportunity of interviewing Mr. Josei Toda, then the Soka Gakkai president. Since that time I have followed developments with keen interest and have written articles on Soka Gakkai both for the *Japan Times* and for publications outside Japan.

During the more than ten years since then, I have seen popular interest in Soka Gakkai rise sharply both inside and outside Japan. I found, however, that persons who were interested in Soka Gakkai were seriously handicapped by the lack of an objectively written account of the organization and its background in Buddhism. This book represents my attempt to fill the void. If it should prove successful in mitigating unfounded fears of Soka Gakkai or ignorance about it, then I shall be well content.

In the process of writing the book, I found formidable the task of explaining the esoteric in exoteric terms, of making intelligible some of the most profound aspects of Buddhist philosophy as interpreted by Nichiren Shoshu and Soka Gakkai. Fortunately, I received generous assistance from many officers of Soka Gakkai, who gave me much of their time and also read the manuscript and made a number of corrections of fact and suggestions for improvement. I am particularly indebted to President Daisaku Ikeda, who patiently tried to elucidate the doctrines of Nichiren Shoshu over many hours, provided me with a large quantity of pertinent literature and photographs, and also wrote the Foreword to this book. Mr. Tomiya Akiyama, director of Soka Gakkai's Foreign Affairs

Bureau, likewise gave me much invaluable assistance. Whatever errors of fact or misunderstandings of doctrine this book
may still contain, therefore, are entirely my own.

Finally, I should like to thank Mr. Meredith Weatherby,
editor-in-chief of John Weatherhill, Inc., for first suggesting
that I write this book. The experience has been one from which
I have learned enormously.

Three small notes on matters of style: 1) In several instances
of Soka Gakkai's technical vocabulary, I have taken the liberty
of departing from their approved style in favor of one that
will, I hope, be easier for the general reader. Hence, instead
of "Sokagakkai" I use the more usual journalistic form "Soka
Gakkai"; instead of "Honzon" and "Gohonzon," the forms
that indicate the special reverence that followers of Nichiren
have for these sacred objects, I use the more generic forms
honzon and *gohonzon;* and instead of "Nam-myoho-renge-kyo,"
the form that emphasizes the indivisibility of this sacred
phrase, I have chosen to break it up for easier reading as
"Nam-myoho Renge-kyo." 2) The names of all modern (post-
1868) Japanese in the book are given in Western style (surname last), while those of premodern Japanese appear in
Japanese style (surname first). 3) All dates prior to November
8, 1872, are by the lunar calendar; on that day Japan changed
from the lunar to the Gregorian calendar.

A word of semantic caution seems called for. According to
Nichiren Shoshu, the term "Lotus Sutra," which corresponds
to "Hoke-kyo" in Japanese, has three different meanings.
They are 1) the twenty-eight-chapter Sanskrit sutra which is
held to carry preachings by the historical Buddha, 2) the
Mo-ho Chih-kuan by China's Chih-i (see page 45), and 3) the
sacred phrase "Nam-myoho Renge-kyo," which is the quintessence of the doctrine of the Nichiren Shoshu sect itself and
is equated with the *sandai hiho* ("the three great secret
laws"—see pages 51–55). To Nichiren Shoshu, therefore, the
third is the only important meaning of the term "Lotus Sutra." Whenever it is used in relation to the activities of
Nichiren, Nichiren Shoshu, or Soka Gakkai, it carries this
meaning.

Japan's New Buddhism

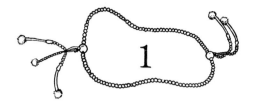

Soka Gakkai in Action

On October 15, 1967, the National Stadium in Tokyo—the site of the 1964 Olympic Games—was the setting for an even more spectacular event, the Tokyo Culture Festival. On a scale appropriate to the world's largest metropolis, vast, symbolic panoramas were portrayed in the synchronized movements of some 42,000 persons, watched by 10,000 awed spectators. Nowhere on the program or posters was there any mention of the organizers of the event: Soka Gakkai, an association of lay adherents of a Japanese Buddhist sect. Yet, to members and nonmembers alike, this display of mass cohesion and discipline was a formidable demonstration of the power and potential of Soka Gakkai.

Precisely at one o'clock in the afternoon, 150 rockets were fired, like a gun salute, into the cloudless skies to signal the opening of the program. At that instant, the vast rectangular space in the stands facing the grandstand turned into a huge curtain of thirteen horizontal colored stripes. To a fanfare relayed by three powerful loudspeaker systems—widely spaced for stereophonic effect—the curtain opened from the center to reveal a gigantic Mount Fuji standing against a sky of changing hue.

The beating wings of five thousand pigeons released simultaneously broke the hush of the stunned spectators. By the time the pigeons were out of sight, sparkling red characters reading "Tokyo Culture Festival" had appeared on the mammoth screen.

What stunned the audience was the fact that the enormous, changing panorama consisted of 42,000 young men and women. Throughout the two hours and fifty-five minutes of the program, each served as a single spot of color on a huge "canvas" three hundred meters wide at the top, two hundred meters wide at the bottom, and fifty meters high—the dimensions of the stadium's bleachers occupied by the human brush strokes.

Each person faithfully followed the signals given by a controller with a set of numbered flags and electric bulbs on top of the opposite grandstand. At every signal, each person raised one of thirteen colored flash cards, according to a predetermined code.

All together, 350 different panoramas were presented. Some symbolized the organization's aims and spiritual values—for example, pictures of Mount Fuji, the eagle (suggesting the vigor of the Youth Division), the enormous hall of worship to be built at Taiseki-ji temple, etc. There were also patterns taken from famous woodblock prints of old Japanese masters; there were even pictures of Occidental heritage (works of Van Gogh, Manet, and Renoir, among others) as well as such internationally famous sights as the Colosseum, the Tower of London, and Venice. For diversion there were also cartoon characters popular with youngsters.

Toward the end came a series of characters meaning "world peace," written in eleven languages—Japanese, English, Russian, Hindi, German, Spanish, Vietnamese, Chinese, Italian, Arabic, and French, in that order.

A unique achievement was the animation of the human panorama. The parting of the "curtain" at the opening, for instance, was effected by thirty thousand persons responding to a series of forty-three signals given at half-second intervals. During the first half of the program, thirty thousand persons were used, and later twelve thousand were added to achieve the effect of a cinema screen of conventional dimensions being extended to Cinemascope proportions.

The human-canvas scheme called for superhuman efforts at all levels of production. First the patterns had to be drawn and painted. The was done by 210 members of the Art Division of Soka Gakkai, which included professional artists of both Occidental and Japanese styles, motion-picture animators, graphic designers, and interior decorators. Because its members come from all walks of life, Soka Gakkai suffers from no dearth of

The Tokyo Culture Festival

October 15, 1967

1. As the Tokyo Culture Festival opens, the flash-card manipulators in the stands create a gigantic Mount Fuji, and five thousand pigeons are released.

2. *Members of the Young Men's Division present a gymnastic performance against a flash-card background depicting an eagle—symbol of Soka Gakkai's youth group.*

*3. After the finale of their performance, young gymnasts wave
to the spectators.*

4. *Quick-changing sequences of flash-card patterns picture a ship being tossed by high waves—a suggestion of the arduous road ahead for Soka Gakkai in its conversion drive.*

5. *The 2,000-member Young Women's Division offers ballet and modern-dance numbers.*

6. *Gymnastic performance by members of the Young Men's Division.*

8. *As the festival ends, young participants cele-*
brate its success with shouts of joy.

7. *Members of the Women's Division, in traditional costume, perform folk dances while the flash-card background appropriately pictures classical woodblock prints.*

9. *For the grand finale, the characters for "world peace" are inscribed on the human canvas in the stands. The handwriting is that of President Ikeda.*

professional skill of any kind for its numerous undertakings.

The team began preparation of the patterns in mid-June 1967. The designs submitted by the various artists were studied by a committee. Many of them were rejected, and more patterns were drawn. The dimensions of the bleacher space as seen from the "royal box" of the grandstand were scaled down to manageable proportions: thirty-five centimeters high and three meters wide. None of the artists had ever painted on such an elongated canvas.

Much effort went into the preparation of the designs. An artist assigned to draw patterns of the eagle, for instance, studied documentary films, consulted books in libraries, and waited for a whole day at a zoo for an eagle to take to the air so that he might be able to acquire a realistic image of the bird in flight. For the four frames that showed the Grand Main Temple to be built at Taiseki-ji temple, more than one hundred sketches were needed. The twenty quick-changing frames that gave the illusion of fireworks bursting in the sky resulted from more than two hundred patterns drawn by fifty artists.

Once the designs were chosen, each of the total of about three hundred pictures was drawn and painted over a canvas thirty-five centimeters high and three meters wide, divided into either 30,000 or 42,000 squares. In each picture, every square had to be filled with one of the thirteen colors. At the rate of three seconds to fill one square, it took thirty-five hours to paint a single frame.

The pattern was then cut into many pieces and divided among the units or "blocks" of Soka Gakkai members making up the "canvas." Leaders of each block then prepared a list of numbers for each of its members, indicating what color card was to be raised at what signal. Each block member was assigned a particular seat in the 42,000-seat "canvas" in the stands. Each participant had then to practice raising the correct color card at the right moment.

For weeks before the Culture Festival, each block usually practiced at night on public-school grounds or on a river embankment—the latter providing a slope simulating the stadium bleachers. The same was true of the preparations for all other aspects of the program: the members were working people who had to use off-work hours. Members of the Women's Division, who were mostly housewives, assembled for practice between household chores.

The entire group of 42,000 conducted rehearsals on four occasions at the National Stadium prior to the big day. Each individual's thirteen cardboard cards were in the following colors: red, gold, pink, yellow, light green, green, silver, light blue, dark blue, beige, sepia, white, and brown. Each card was seventy-five centimeters by forty-three centimeters, with a rectangular slit eighteen centimeters wide and three centimeters high toward the top to enable its holder to see the signals.

The spectacular color effect of the cardboard panorama was due largely to the care that had gone into the preparation of pigments for the various hues. After the boards had been painted, each was given a glossy coating.

At the National Stadium, the signals were given in two stages. First the flag indicated the number for a particular picture to be presented. Then the three yellow bulbs in the row of five were lit to allow the card carriers time to select the right card. When the fourth, a blue bulb, went on, the cards were to be raised. They were lowered when the fifth, a red bulb, was lit after the blue bulb blinked as a warning.

Although the human panorama was a performance of colossal proportions in itself, it was only a part of the entire Culture Festival. It served as a backdrop for the programs unfolded in the arena of the stadium, where large groups formed patterns in synchronized motion—called in Japan "mass games." The program began with a performance entitled "Jubilation" by two thousand members of the Young Women's Division. In the flowing, rhythmic movements of modern dance and classical ballet—accentuated by their colored veils—they formed complex moving patterns: large circles, small circles, and symbolic figures. The choreography had been composed by a man-and-wife team of professional dancers who are members of Soka Gakkai.

The next item was heralded by a huge red eagle on the human backdrop, symbol of the Young Men's Division of Soka Gakkai, which presented with 1,440 of its members a mass-gymnastics display entitled "Fighting Spirit." Their bodies naked to the waist, they entered the arena with the traditional shout of "Wasshoi! wasshoi!" The tanned torsos testified to the frequent practices they had had over the previous two months. In sharp contrast to the feminine grace of the opening number, this was characterized by youthful vigor and strength as the performers leapt and sprang with agile precision.

As the young men left the arena in receding waves of white and brown, a Mount Fuji appeared on the backdrop to the strains of a traditional Japanese melody. Four thousand two hundred women in colorful kimono entered to present "Japanese Tide"—popular folk dances accompanied by familiar songs.

"Waves of the World" followed: a musical program featuring a 650-man brass band, a 2,270-member fife-and-drum corps, and a "junior corps" of primary-school girls with accordions and drums. Then came "Youthful Force," gymnastics by 1,500 high-school boys, and "Construction" by 2,640 members of the Men's Division and 2,310 members of the Women's Division.

This entire program, with its tens of thousands of performers, went without a hitch, although there were no signals or prompters. The music alone supplied the cues that insured continuity.

Such a streamlined professional performance on such a scale was all the more remarkable for the fact that all the participants were amateurs with only three months' rehearsal experience behind them. They were white-collar workers, factory hands, cooks, carpenters, garage mechanics, high-school students, and housewives. To each one, his role in the event, however humble, was a coveted privilege and honor, dispensed only to a small fraction of the entire membership of Soka Gakkai.

What, then, are the factors that lie behind such a spontaneous *espirit de corps?*

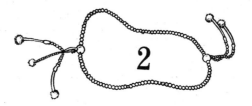

A Brief Outline

In approaching a subject as complex and esoteric as Soka Gakkai, perhaps it will be helpful to the reader to have a brief outline, a hurried bird's-eye view of the terrain that lies ahead. The present chapter, then, is in the nature of a preview of the entire book. Each point presented here will be treated in detail in the succeeding chapters.

Soka Gakkai members are lay adherents of the Buddhist sect called Nichiren Shoshu, meaning literally "the orthodox sect of Nichiren." Nichiren was a Buddhist evangelist of the thirteenth century who preached salvation through faith in the seven-character holy phrase "Nam-myoho Renge-kyo." Literally, this means "Devotion to the Wonderful Law Lotus Sutra," the sutra in this case being the Mahayana Buddhist scripture called (in Sanskrit) the Saddharma Pundarika Sutra. According to the doctrine of Nichiren Shoshu, this phrase in itself, not the Lotus Sutra, is the basic scripture of the sect.

Shortly after Nichiren's death, one of his chief disciples, Nikko, broke with the other five and left the temple of Kuon-ji at Minobu, Nichiren's last base for evangelical activities. While the other disciples formed the Nichiren Shu (Nichiren sect), with Kuon-ji as head temple, Nikko formed a sect of his own based on a different interpretation of his mentor's teaching from that of the other disciples. One of the branches of this sect later came to be known as Nichiren Shoshu, whose head temple is Taiseki-ji at Fujinomiya, near Mount Fuji.

The two sects remain rivals to this day, but it is only recently that Nichiren Shoshu has won more adherents than Nichiren Shu, thanks largely to Soka Gakkai's conversion activities. Some three million pilgrims now visit the head temple annually, almost all of them Soka Gakkai members. All together, more than three hundred Nichiren Shoshu temples are found throughout Japan and in other countries, and all are subordinate to Taiseki-ji.

Soka Gakkai itself had its origins in 1930 when a Tokyo schoolteacher, Tsunesaburo Makiguchi, founded Soka Kyoiku Gakkai (Value-Creating Educational Academic Society). Makiguchi based the society's program on a combination of Nichiren Shoshu theology and his own theory of value. He held that there are three ultimate virtues: *bi* (beauty), *ri* (gain), and *zen* (goodness). The purpose of life, he maintained, is the pursuit of happiness, which lies in the attainment of the three supreme virtues, and they in turn are accessible only through faith in the teaching of Nichiren.

The goal the believers in Nichiren Shoshu aim to attain is *kosen rufu,* literally, "the spreading abroad of Buddhism"—that is, Nichiren Shoshu, which is claimed to be the only "true Buddhism." This belief is based on their own interpretation of Nichiren's teachings.

Uncompromising belief in Nichiren Shoshu as the only true faith brought persecution to members of Soka Kyoiku Gakkai in the 1940's. The ultranationalistic regime of the day tried to subordinate all other religious groups to the state religion of Shinto, and in 1943, when Soka Kyoiku Gakkai leaders still refused to accept the supremacy of Shinto, they were jailed. Many members had renounced their faith, and, with the leaders gone, the association ceased to exist. Founder Makiguchi died in detention in 1944, but his principal disciple, Josei Toda (also a schoolteacher), survived despite his steadfast refusal to accept the Shinto faith. Released in July 1945, Toda revived the association in early 1946, renaming it Soka Gakkai (Value-Creating Academic Society). He served as *rijicho* (chairman of its board of directors), while the office of *kaicho* (president),[1] formerly held by Makiguchi, was left open until 1951, when Toda took up the post as a full-time occupation.

Once he had become president, Toda devoted his energies to winning converts to Soka Gakkai as a step toward the ultimate goal of *kosen rufu.* The association adopted a traditional

---

[1] In Soka Gakkai, in contrast with business corporations, the president, not the chairman of the board, is the highest officer.

Buddhist method of proselytizing called *shakubuku*, which is characterized by its activism, but members pursued it with such zeal as to arouse considerable criticism and ill feeling. Nevertheless, the intensive drive for membership was eminently successful, for Soka Gakkai membership skyrocketed from 3,000 families in mid-1951 to 765,000 families at the end of 1957.

President Toda died in 1958, and in 1960 his trusted disciple Daisaku Ikeda became third president of the association. Under Ikeda, Soka Gakkai has continued to expand both its membership and its range of activities. In early 1969, it boasted a membership of 6,876,000 households. For these members as well as other citizens who are considered to be potential members, the association organizes religious, cultural, and educational activities. Every day about fifteen thousand Soka Gakkai members from all over Japan and from abroad visit the temple Taiseki-ji, the mecca of Nichiren Shoshu. The pilgrimages are arranged to a carefully detailed schedule by volunteer members of the Transportation Section, directed by the Pilgrimage Department of the association's headquarters.

At Taiseki-ji, the visitors are given an opportunity to view the Daigohonzon ("great object of worship"): the sacred tablet on which Nichiren's own writing of the holy phrase "Nam-myoho Renge-kyo" is inscribed. This wooden tablet is a chief basis of Nichiren Shoshu's claim to orthodoxy in the succession of Nichiren's teachings.

One of Soka Gakkai's nonreligious affiliates is the Min'on Concert Association, whose programs are open to the general public as well as to members. It sponsors concerts and ballets at relatively low cost. Another is the Min'en Theatrical Association, which likewise stages plays.

Soka Gakkai is also keen to provide its own educational programs, which is not coincidental, because the association started out as an educational society and its first two presidents were schoolteachers. In the spring of 1968, Soka Gakkai's lower and upper secondary schools were opened, and plans are under way to open a university in 1971.

The association's most important secular activity is in politics. Soka Gakkai's own political party, Komeito (Clean Government Party), was formally inaugurated in 1964 and has participated in both national and local elections since then with remarkable success. As of January 1969, it had twenty-four seats in the 250-seat House of Councilors (the upper house of the National Diet) and twenty-five seats in the 486-seat House of Representatives. Komeito candidates also held 1,982 seats in local legislatures throughout Japan.

While Soka Gakkai's program of conversion, *kosen rufu*, is its primary concern, the ultimate goal of universality has been modified by Ikeda to the conversion of one-third of the population of Japan by 1979. The year is the seven-hundredth anniversary of the year in which Nichiren is said to have "endowed the world with the Daigohonzon"—1279. Seven is an auspicious number in Oriental numerology, and 1979 has further significance as the twenty-first anniversary of Toda's death in 1958. (Twenty-one, as a multiple of seven, is also regarded as an auspicious number.)

Soka Gakkai leaders make much use of numerology in their interpretation and planning of events. For example, they attach great significance to the fact that Nichiren founded his sect in 1253, almost exactly seven hundred years after the introduction of Buddhism to Japan (in A.D. 552, according to one of Japan's oldest written records).

Deeper religious significance is also found in events through Nichiren Shoshu's theory of history. The concept central to this theory is that of *mappo*, the Japanese equivalent of the Sankskrit *saddharma vipralopa* (literally, "the extinction of the right law"), meaning, in Nichiren Shoshu terms, "extinction of the teaching of the historical Buddha." According to certain Buddhist sutras, the effect of the Buddha's teaching would slowly wane in the centuries after his death. During the first ten centuries, the period of *shoho* (also *shobo:* right law), his teachings would remain effective enough to save those who practiced them. In the next ten centuries, the period of *zoho* (also *zobo:* false law), people's faith would lack substance, although the Buddha's influence would not be extinct. But in the third millennium the world was to enter the period of *mappo*, when the Buddha's teachings would cease to be effective and all hope of salvation would be lost.

Japanese Buddhists accept 949 B.C. as the year of the Buddha's death, so they date the era of *mappo* from A.D. 1051.

As if to bear out their eschatology, many natural disasters and civil disturbances are recorded after this date. In Nichiren's own lifetime, in the thirteenth century, Buddhism, after seven hundred years in Japan, was indeed corrupt and decadent, and the Buddhist priesthood seemed incapable of reform. Yet, according to the sutras, it was in this period of depravity that the savior, a reincarnation of the eternal Buddha, was to appear. His teaching alone, not that of the historical Buddha, would open the way to salvation.

Nichiren's followers claim that his observation of society and his study of sutras, particularly of the Lotus Sutra, convinced him that he was this savior. Sure of his mission, Nichiren withstood the jealousy and persecution of other Buddhist groups. He prophesied to the Hojos, the warrior clan then in political control of Japan, that unless the nation declared its faith in the Lotus Sutra it would suffer a terrible catastrophe, such as conquest by a foreign power. Shortly thereafter, Kublai Khan's Mongol army tried unsuccessfully to invade Kyushu, the westernmost island of Japan. For Nichiren, the event bore out his prophecy and confirmed him in his sacred mission. He spent the rest of his life preaching faith in the Lotus Sutra, and despite persecution—including exile and attempts to execute or assassinate him—he survived to the age of sixty and died in 1282.

Seven centuries after his death, Nichiren has in Soka Gakkai and Nichiren Shoshu a well-organized following to carry out the task he embarked upon: the spreading of the canon of the Lotus Sutra throughout Japan and the world. But Nichiren's present-day disciples are far better equipped to spread the faith than were those of the thirteenth century. They have at their disposal all the technological achievements of the twentieth century in transport and communications. In Nichiren's time, every copy of a sutra or a book had to be laboriously transcribed by hand. A speech or a sermon reached the ears of only a small crowd. Today, Soka Gakkai thrives primarily on the sale of the books it publishes for members and even for nonmembers. A leader can address and influence thousands of people at a time. And, even more important, while Nichiren could press his cause to the rulers of the land only by submitting a memorial, Soka Gakkai today can seek to influence the government with much greater success through its own political party, Komeito.

Obviously the future development of Soka Gakkai is a matter of great interest and importance not only to Japan and the Japanese but also, given the shrinking size of the world, to people everywhere.

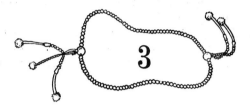

The History
of Nichiren Shoshu

THE BUDDHIST BACKGROUND

Because Soka Gakkai is an association of lay adherents of a Buddhist sect, any discussion of it must rest on an understanding of Buddhism itself.

Gautama Siddhartha, the Buddha (literally, "the enlightened one"), known in Japan as Shakamuni (Sakyamuni), lived in India in the sixth century B.C. and during his lifetime won a great number of disciples to his teachings. About a century after his death, his following split over different interpretations of his teachings. By the beginning of the Christian era, two major sects had emerged. One called itself Mahayana (Greater Vehicle) and referred belittlingly to its chief rival as Hinayana (Lesser Vehicle), better known by its own designation, Theravada, meaning "the School of the Elders."

Theravada Buddhism spread to Ceylon, Burma, Thailand, Laos, and Cambodia, while Mahayana found its way to China, Tibet, Korea, and then to Japan. Briefly, Theravada reveres the teachings of the historical Buddha. This religion is primarily a way of life which offers release to the individual from the sufferings of human life by helping him attain tranquility of mind. A Theravadist seeks the goal of enlightenment by faithful adherence to the rule of conduct, the Eightfold Path, set down by the Buddha.

Mahayana, on the other hand, deified the historical Buddha, regarding him as one particular incarnation of the eternal,

22

transcendent Buddha nature. Against the quietism of Hinayana, with its emphasis on personal abnegation, is set the
activism of Mahayana, concerned with the salvation of all
mankind. Hence the term "Greater Vehicle"—a means of
transporting a larger number of individuals to the realm of
supreme enlightenment. To Mahayanists, Theravada Buddhism
was like a vehicle that accommodated only one person.

Theravada and Mahayana also differ in their respective use
of the word bodhisattva (a person who seeks enlightenment).
In Theravada, bodhisattva meant Gautama the Buddha in his
previous incarnation, during which he performed many acts of
merit. It was because of these acts of merit, according to
Theravada, that Gautama was able to become a Buddha, an
"enlightened one," in his actual life.

The Mahayanists, however, believed that they themselves
could become Buddhas through their own endeavor and that
therefore they should be called bodhisattvas. They expected a
bodhisattva both to live righteously and to save others spiritu-
ally. He was to become a Buddha by working for the good of
others through perfecting himself in the six virtues of
generosity, morality, patience, vigor, meditative concentration,
and wisdom.

In such an endeavor, however, the Mahayanist also depended
on the aid of transcendent Buddhas and bodhisattvas (who
delay their own attainment of Buddhahood to assist others).
Examples of the latter are Amitabha (Amida Nyorai in
Japanese) and Avalokitesvara (Kanzeon Bosatsu in Japanese).

Another characteristic of Mahayana Buddhism was that it
produced a vast number of sutras which purport to record the
Buddha's actual teachings. Buddhist scholars believe that these
sutras were compiled during the centuries before and after the
year A.D. 1.

THE LOTUS SUTRA

The holy scripture of Nichiren sects (as well as the Tendai
sect of Japanese Buddhism), is the sutra of Mahayana
Buddhism known in Sanskrit as the Saddharma Pundarika
Sutra, which means literally the "Lotus Right Law Sutra."

The prefix *sat (sad)*, the present participle of a verb which means "to exist," is used in the sense of "present," "existing," "true," "wonderful," "right," or "superior." *Dharma* means "law" or "teaching." *Saddharma* was therefore translated into Chinese by one translator as *miao fa* (*myoho* in Japanese), the two ideographs meaning "wonderful" and "law," and into *sheng fa* by another. This phrase, pronounced *shoho* in Japanese, means "right law."

Pundarika, on the other hand, means "white lotus," and the compound *saddharma pundarika* is understood to mean "the right law which is like the white lotus." The lotus is an important Buddhist symbol of purity and spiritual merit. It is used extensively as a symbolic ornament in Buddhist architecture. Artificial white lotus blossoms are always found in Buddhist funeral decorations. Soka Gakkai's theoretical publication is entitled *Daibyakurenge* (Great White Lotus Blossom). The name Nichiren means literally "sun lotus."

Most scholars agree that the Lotus Sutra was compiled over a long period of time by many students and practitioners of Buddhism. Some fix the period when the sutra was written between A.D. 40 and 220. The consensus among scholars is that the prototype of the Lotus Sutra predated the birth of Christ. It emerged from an assembly of laymen who were protesting against the priesthood's interpretation and practice of the Buddha's teaching. In praise of their great teacher, these bodhisattvas composed verses to express their personal faith. Over the centuries further expressions of faith were added to the original to form the Lotus Sutra. One of the foremost scholars of Buddhism and an authority on the Lotus Sutra, Shoko Watanabe, says that the sutra was known at the beginning of the Christian era in various forms in different regions of northwestern India. When the first known texts of the sutra were compiled, several versions already existed.[1]

Today, there are three Sanskrit texts of the sutra, known respectively as the Nepalese, Central Asian, and Gilgit texts, after the places where they were discovered. According to Yutaka Iwamoto, another Sanskrit scholar and authority on the sutra, only the Nepalese version is complete. The Nepalese

[1] Shoko Watanabe: "Shokai Shin'yaku Hoke-kyo" (A Comprehensive New Translation of the Lotus Sutra), *Daihorin*, February 1968, pp. 58–67.

text was discovered by Brian Houghton Hodgson (1800–1866), a British diplomat and Orientalist stationed in Nepal. Emile Louis Burnouf (1821–44), a French Orientalist who received the text of the Lotus Sutra from Hodgson, produced a French translation which was published posthumously in 1852 by his pupils under the title of *Le Lotus de la Bonne Loi*. In 1909, Jan Hendrik Kern (1833–1917) produced an English translation entitled *The Saddharma-pundarika or the Lotus of the True Law*. In collaboration with Bun'yu Nanjo, a Japanese scholar who had studied Sanskrit under the famous philologist Friedrich Max Müller, Kern edited the first Sanskrit publication of the sutra. It was published in St. Petersburg between 1908 and 1912 as part of the fifty-one-volume series called *Sacred Books of the East*. Three more versions in Sanskrit were published, all based on the Kern-Nanjo edition, which is considered the basic text of the sutra today. Iwamoto published a Japanese version of the sutra on the basis of this Sanskrit edition.[2]

The sutra is presented mainly in the form of a discourse by the Buddha to his followers, as recorded by Ananda, the Buddha's cousin and close disciple. It presents the historical Buddha as an immortal, idealized being. In mythical allegories, fables, and verses, the sutra glorifies the supernatural powers and prowess of the Buddha. References to "tens of millions of persons," "thousands of worlds," and "eons upon eons of time" heighten the fantasy, whose *dramatis personae* are not mere mortals but divine beings—bodhisattvas and Buddhas. The cosmic drama thus unfolded presents Buddhism as a pantheistic religion despite its origin as a strictly nontheistic faith.

Because the Lotus Sutra was composed over a long span of time, it is not always consistent. Its power to inspire the serious reader lies in the religious fervor which animates the sutra—hence its key position in Buddhist literature and in the history of Oriental thought. Undoubtedly, it is the most influential and important of all the Mahayana scriptures. In

[2] Yutaka Iwamoto and Yukio Sakamoto: *Hoke-kyo* (The Lotus Sutra), 3 vols., Iwanami Shoten, Tokyo, 1962–67. This edition consists of two texts of the sutra: a translation from Sanskrit by Iwamoto and a translation from Chinese by Sakamoto, which are printed on facing pages for contrast and comparison.

Japan, the title of the sutra, Hoke-kyo (an abbreviation of Myoho Renge-kyo), is a household word—so familiar that the onomatopoeia for the call of the nightingale in Japanese is *ho-hoke-kyo.*

A chief characteristic of the Lotus Sutra is its insistence upon its absolute supremacy over all other sutras. It claims to be the verbal expression of the supreme philosophy of the historical Buddha. Furthermore, it assures anyone who commits himself to the sutra of infinite moral and physical benefits and of eventual Buddhahood. At the same time, the sutra warns the faithful that they are bound to be persecuted in their attempts to propagate it. Nevertheless, those who fail to proselytize and those who persecute the faithful will receive divine retribution.

The Lotus Sutra known in Japan is a Chinese version, which is read in two ways. In one, the original Chinese pronunciation, as Japanized through the centuries, is followed. In the other, the Chinese syntax is translated into Japanese—the usual manner in which Japanese "read" Chinese classics. Although several Chinese translations of the original text were made during the early centuries, the principal one, which is almost the only version known and read in Japan today, is the text produced by Kumarajiva (350–409), the Sino-Indian scholar known in Japan as Kumaraju.

Kumarajiva is said to have been a descendant of a succession of prime ministers of an Indian province. However, his father, a prime minister, gave up the post and became a Buddhist monk. While at Kucha (in the Sinkiang-Uigur Autonomous Region of modern China), he had married the sister of the local king, and Kumarajiva was their son. His mother became a Buddhist nun, and Kumarajiva himself joined the priesthood at the age of seven.

When he was eight, Kumarajiva accompanied his mother to Kashmir, where he studied Theravada. Later, when he studied Mahayana Buddhism, Kumarajiva became convinced of its superiority over the Hinayana version. In A.D. 401, after a checkered career, he settled in Ch'angan, today's Sian (in Shensi Province), then the most important city of China. For nine years, until his death in 409, Kumarajiva devoted himself to the monumental task of translating Buddhist scriptures

from Sanskrit into Chinese. With the assistance of his colleagues and pupils, he is said to have translated a total of 384
volumes of sutras. Nevertheless, he paid special attention to
the translation of the Lotus Sutra, supervising the work of
five hundred priest-translators.

The king whom Kumarajiva served was concerned that this
great scholar, celibate because he was a priest, would leave no
children. Anxious that Kumarajiva should produce offspring
of equal intellect, the king removed him from the monastery to
laymen's living quarters, where Kumarajiva lived with ten
beautiful women. Having obeyed the king's wishes, Kumarajiva
apparently felt guilty about the coerced act of apostasy, for he
declared: "I am ignorant, and furthermore I translated the
sutras with my impure body. When I die, cremate me. If my
translations are all correct, then my tongue will not burn, even
if my body does. But if my tongue should burn, destroy all
the translations I made."

Legend has it that when he died at the age of fifty-nine, his
body was cremated, and the tongue alone did not burn but
radiated light in five colors at night.

The Chinese received Kumarajiva's translation of the Lotus
Sutra with great favor, and it was read and used widely. Chih-i
(538–97) founded his T'ien-t'ai sect on the basis of this sutra.
Two centuries later, the Japanese Buddhist Saicho (767–822)
established the Japanese version of China's T'ien-t'ai sect—
the Tendai sect—after studying the Lotus Sutra according to
Chih-i's doctrines.

Scholars comparing Kumarajiva's version with the Sanskrit
original have found many discrepancies between the two. Shoko
Watanabe points out that Kumarajiva's translation of the
Sanskrit original was fairly free so as to make the sutra easily
comprehensible to Chinese readers. Perhaps as a result, the
literary style of Kumarajiva's version contributes to the impact
the sutra has on the reader.

Another feature of the Lotus Sutra is the zeal, occasionally
bordering on fanaticism, it has generated in its followers. To
some zealous devotees of the sutra, all else, including life itself,
came only second to the sutra. Unlike the meditative approach
of the monks to the sutra, that of some of the lay believers
was activist, totally committed to what they understood was

the true teaching of the Buddha. Some took a literal interpretation of the sutra. In Chapter 23, entitled "Yakuobosatsu
Honjihon" (The Previous Life of Bhaisajyaraja),[3] is an
allegory in which a bodhisattva named Sarvasattvapriyadarsana[4] (Issaishujokikenbosatsu in Japanese) offers his
thanksgiving for his enlightenment after 12,000 years of hard
practice. He drinks several fragrant balms for twelve years
(1,200 years according to the Chinese version of the sutra)
and then ignites himself. The light emanating from his burning
body illumined, according to the sutra's literal meaning, worlds
"whose number was the same as that of the sands of eighty
Ganges Rivers"—an infinite number. The bodhisattva's body,
says the sutra, continued to burn for 1,200 years. In the same
chapter there is a reference to another devotee who offered
his own arm, which was lit, and it too burned for 72,000 years.

In ancient China, some devotees took these allegories literally
and burned their fingers or arms and even incinerated themselves in drastic affirmation of their faith.[5] And to early
followers of the Lotus Sutra in Japan, such acts of devotion
were thought more important than the intellectual compre-
hension of the sutra.

NICHIREN AND HIS LIFE

Among the world's religious leaders Nichiren distinguished
himself by the large number of writings he left. There are
more than seven hundred extant writings of his, of which
nearly five hundred are complete. Many are copies of lost
original texts, but there are 115 complete texts preserved in
the original and 328 incomplete items. Nichiren did not
produce major works like those of a few other Buddhist leaders
of medieval Japan; he wrote many short treatises and a vast

[3] Bhaisajyaraja means "king of medicine."
[4] Sarvasattvapriyadarsana means "person whose figure is liked by all
people."
[5] When in the 1960's several Buddhist priests and nuns of South Viet-
nam burned themselves in what appeared to be a gesture of protest
against a government they strongly disapproved of, some of the Japanese Buddhists interpreted the instances as acts of self-immolation—that
is, the persons concerned had offered their supreme gift—their own bodies
—to the Buddha in beseeching him to save their country.

number of letters to his lay patrons and followers throughout his career, reflecting the development of his thought at every stage.

Nichiren recorded that he was the son of a poor fisherman at Kominato in today's Chiba Prefecture of eastern Japan. He described himself as "a person of the indigent and lowest class," from a *sendara* family (*sendara* is the Japanese cognate of the Sanskrit word *cendala*, meaning one of the untouchable Indian castes, namely that of the slaughterers). His allusion to a *sendara* may reflect the low status of fishermen of thirteenth-century Japan, or it may be Nichiren's exaggeration of his plebeian background. However, few people today accept the theory of various eighteenth- and nineteenth-century biographers of Nichiren who, out of reverence for him, maintained that Nichiren was descended from a samurai who was related to the imperial family.

Indeed, Nichiren's present-day disciples, including Soka Gakkai members, proudly stress the importance, from the Buddhist angle, of Nichiren's humble birth. For Nichiren Shoshu adherents in particular, who regard Nichiren as the earthly embodiment of the eternal Buddha, he seems all the greater for having been born a commoner rather than a prince, as the historical Buddha was. Clearly, Nichiren himself felt his achievement to be all the higher because of his lowly origins.

A biography of Nichiren written by Nichido, the fourth-generation high priest of Nichiren Shoshu, claims that Nichiren was born on February 16, 1222. Historians, however, find no evidence for this. Some hold that Nichido chose it arbitrarily because, according to Japanese Buddhist tradition, Gautama the Buddha died on February 15. In other words, the biographer felt it appropriate that Nichiren, regarded as the contemporary heir to the historical Buddha, should have been born on the day after the anniversary of the Buddha's death.

At the age of twelve, the boy Nichiren, known as Zennichimaro, was entrusted to the care of the priest Dozembo of Seicho-ji temple (known also as Kiyosumi Temple) in his home town. At sixteen, he entered the priesthood with the priestly name of Zenshobo. As Seicho-ji temple belonged to the Tendai sect, Nichiren studied its canon, but he also studied the doctrines of the Shingon sect, another major school of Buddhism in Japan at the time.

Later, Nichiren journeyed from Kominato in pursuit of further knowledge of Buddhism. At Kamakura, his first stop, he studied the canons of the Jodo and Zen sects. After a return to Seicho-ji temple, he went farther west to Mount Hiei, the mecca of the Tendai sect, and then to Mount Koya, the home of the Shingon sect, as well as to other temples in the region—mostly in Kyoto and Nara.

Following travels for about ten years, seeking knowledge, he returned home, and on April 28, 1253, at Seicho-ji, at the age of thirty-one, he revealed the result of the years of his study. His followers believe that on this day Nichiren uttered the phrase "Nam-myoho Renge-kyo" (Devotion to the Lotus Sutra), as the quintessence of the absolute truth of Buddhism. He then enunciated the famous four-part maxim *(shiko kakugen)*: 1) Those who believe in Nembutsu sects (according to which salvation lies in reciting the name of the bodhisattva Amitabha) will go to Avici, the inferno of continuous punishment. 2) Those who believe in Zen are devils. 3) The believers in the Shingon sect will ruin the nation. 4) The believers in the Ritsu sect are traitors.

Nichiren meant that the canon of every other Buddhist sect was fake, and they must accept the supremacy of his own Buddhist canon, the Lotus Sutra. But his outspokenness quickly won him enemies. Among them was Tojo Kagenobu, the *jito* (local administrator) for the Hojo regency of Kamakura. As a believer in a Nembutsu sect, Kagenobu was understandably offended by Nichiren's condemnation of all sects other than his own belief. As a result, Nichiren was forced out of Seicho-ji temple and went to Kamakura, where he launched on a career of forthright evangelism.

Nichiren built a hovel at Matsubagayatsu near Kamakura and is said to have engaged in what came to be known popularly as *tsujizeppo* (street-corner preaching). Nichiren Shoshu and Soka Gakkai authorities, however, dispute this as a popular myth, holding that Nichiren conducted personal conversions through group discussions—the prototype of Soka Gakkai's primary *shakubuku* form—rather than impersonal preaching to an outdoor crowd.

Nichiren's ardent evangelizing won him more enemies, but at the same time he was slowly but surely building up a following. However, he had still to undergo a remarkable experience which had a profound impact on his religious belief and his basic outlook on the world.

From 1256, when Nichiren was thirty-four years old, to 1260, Japan was continually subjected to such disasters as earthquakes, storms, droughts, famines, and epidemics. The earthquake that hit Kamakura on August 23, 1257, was particularly disastrous; it demolished homes and left not a single temple or shrine standing. There were also many landslides, and the ground opened up in chasms. Although no precise account is available, casualties must have been tremendous.

A series of disasters also hit the nation throughout 1259, with famine and plague causing large numbers of deaths. There are even records of cannibalism. Nichiren himself recorded at the age of thirty-eight: "In the first year of Shoka (1257), the earth shook much; in the following year, a heavy rainfall washed out rice seedlings in the spring, and a drought in the summer dried up vegetation; a storm in the winter wrecked the harvest, causing a famine that made tens of thousands of refugees."

Likewise he wrote in February 1260 that, from 1257, "earthquakes, unseasonal typhoons, famines, and epidemics came one after another, causing so many deaths that the population appeared to be annihilated." Nichiren prefaced his famous *Rissho Ankoku Ron* (Treatise on Making the Nation Secure by Establishing True Buddhism), which he wrote in 1260, as follows: "From some years ago until recent days, natural disasters, famine, and disease have filled the heavens and the earth and spread throughout the land. Animals have fallen in the streets, and skeletons have filled the city blocks. More than one-half of the population has died, and there is not a single individual who does not mourn the death of kin."

In the midst of this hell on earth, Nichiren wondered about the significance of it all. He was puzzled by the fact that Buddhism, the faith of so many Japanese in numerous sects, apparently could not keep society peaceful and stable nor halt the toll of human suffering. If Buddhism could not save the world, Nichiren wondered, what good was there in it? If the

religions could not end the disasters, then there must be
something wrong with the way the people practiced them.
With this basic doubt in mind, Nichiren decided to renew his
studies of Buddhism.

He left Kamakura on January 6, 1258, for Jisso-ji temple (in
today's Shizuoka Prefecture) to investigate the entire collection of Buddhist sutras and canons available at the temple.
Many years later he wrote that at Jisso-ji he had studied about
five thousand Buddhist documents and about three thousand
non-Buddhist documents. As a result of this intensive research,
Nichiren was able to resolve his doubts and acquire an
unwavering conviction.

THE THEORY OF MAPPO

Fundamental to Nichiren's conviction, as to other Buddhist
leaders of Japan in the twelfth and thirteenth centuries, is the
theory of *mappo,* the last of the three eras of the gradual
decline of Buddhism. The primary source of this theory is the
Mahayana sutra called Daishikkyo (also known as Daijikkyo),
in which the Buddha predicted the extent of the influence
of his teaching in the following three successive periods: 1)
first one thousand years: Era of the Right Law *(shoho* or
shobo), 2) second one thousand years: Era of the False Law
(zoho or *zobo),* and 3) from the 2,001st year on: Era of the
Extinction of the Right Law *(mappo).*

According to the Buddha's prophecy in this sutra, his
teaching would be observed correctly during the first half of
the era of *shoho* and those who practiced Buddhism would
achieve enlightenment. In the latter half of this era, those who
practiced Buddhism were to devote themselves to attaining
tranquility of mind with which to view the truth.

In the first five-hundred-year period of the *zoho* era, the
substance of Buddhism would be lost, and Buddha's teaching
would remain in form only. During the second half of this
period, Buddhism was to be practiced primarily through the
act of constructing temples and pagodas—a sign of formal
rather than genuine religious practice. After two millennia the
true spirit of Buddhism would be extinct (only the form being

THE ERAS OF SHOHO, ZOHO, AND MAPPO

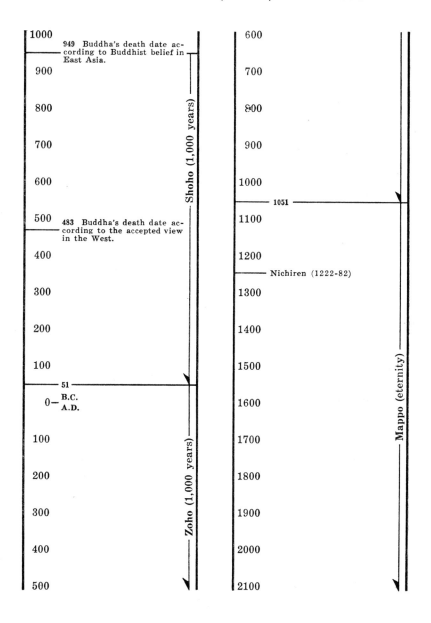

preserved), and the result would be continual deadly strife.

It is obviously vital to know the exact year of the Buddha's death in order to calculate these successive ages, but there are many conflicting theories about the date. According to sutras found in Tibet, he died in 2422 B.C.; according to sutras preserved in Burma, the year was 422 B.C. Buddhists in India, Burma, and Thailand accept the date as 544 B.C. Among Western Orientalists, too, there is no consensus. Nor do contemporary Japanese scholars of Buddhism agree on the death date.

In ancient China and Japan, however, Buddhists held that the Buddha's death had occurred in the year 949 B.C., and it is from this date that the successive eras of *shoho, zoho,* and *mappo* are calculated. As to the length of these three successive eras, there were several theories, the most commonly accepted being that *shoho* and *zoho* last for ten centuries each and *mappo* for ten thousand years—a figure of speech for eternity.

Without this eschatological view of history underlying Japanese Buddhism, there could have been no Nichiren and no Soka Gakkai. According to this view, a true Buddha was destined to appear in the age of *mappo* to save mankind. It is the tenet of Nichiren Shoshu that Nichiren was that savior.

EXHORTATION TO THE GOVERNMENT

Nichiren wrote *Rissho Ankoku Ron* in the form of a dialogue between a guest and his host, using only Chinese characters. In this dialogue the guest represents those who are ignorant of the "right law," the canon of the Lotus Sutra, while the host is evidently the person familiar with it—that is, Nichiren himself. The dialogue has ten sections, each beginning with the guest's question. All the questions except the final, tenth one are followed by the host's answer, the last question being an answer in itself.

The guest asks the host why calamities continue to occur despite Buddhist prayers and rites offered to deities and Buddhas. He is told it is because the nation fails to worship true Buddhism, so the guardian deities have abandoned the land, allowing devils to infest it. Unless the nation makes religious reforms, the disasters will continue indefinitely. The host cites appropriate sutras to back his contention that only nationwide homage to the Lotus Sutra will avert "seven national disasters."

Nichiren believed that five of the seven disasters had already occurred, and, barring acceptance of the Lotus Sutra by the Hojo regency, the two remaining disasters—civil war and foreign invasion—would come also. As a result of this prediction, Nichiren won the reputation of a prophet, for both these disasters actually occurred. The civil war was that of February 1272, when Hojo Tokisuke rebelled; the foreign invasion was that of Kyushu attempted by Mongolia's Kublai Khan in 1274 and again in 1281.

On July 16, 1260, Nichiren submitted his memorial to the regent Hojo Tokiyori, urging him to alter his policy on religion. But Nichiren's proposal proved fruitless, merely resulting in his own persecution. In 1261, at the age of thirty-nine, he was arrested and exiled for about two years.

However, the oppression Nichiren experienced strengthened his spirit of resistance and deepened his commitment to the Lotus Sutra. He came to the conclusion that to preach the canon of the Lotus Sutra in the face of persecution was the true vocation of a devotee of the sutra, as the sutra itself stated. In *Kyokijikokusho*, written in 1261 while he was in exile in Izu, Nichiren declared that a devotee of the Lotus Sutra in the period of *mappo* was destined to encounter "three kinds of formidable enemies," as described in the thirteenth chapter of the sutra. These were 1) persecution by the common masses, 2) persecution by priests of evil religions, and 3) persecution by those who, having received great respect from the masses, pretend to be saints—those who are prominent political leaders.

In this chapter of the sutra there is a scene in which an infinite number of bodhisattvas vow to the Buddha to spread the teaching of the Lotus Sutra. The Buddha tells them that in a "bad era" after his death there will be these three kinds of enemies to harass them, but they should endure the hardship so as to spread the correct faith throughout the world.

When Nichiren cites this particular passage, he seems to be already aware that he is himself the bodhisattva. Belief in his mission ripened when he was exiled to Sado Island in 1271, at the age of forty-nine. The Hojos once again were punishing him for his persistent demands that they accept the Lotus Sutra to save the nation, this time from the threat from Mongolia. Even the circumstances under which he was arrested prior to the exile were such as to heighten Nichiren's sense of mission and of martyrdom.

On September 12, 1271, at about four o'clock in the afternoon, a contingent of several hundred samurai visited Nichiren's abode near Kamakura to arrest him. To the leader of the group, Nichiren declared: "I am the ridgepole and beam of Japan. I am the pillar of Japan. To lose me would mean felling the pillar of the country."

His declaration, however, was of no avail. The soldiers wrecked the room in which Nichiren kept the sutras and Buddhist statues, stepping all over these precious possessions with their muddy feet. They seized a scroll of the Lotus Sutra which Nichiren had concealed in the bosom of his kimono and flailed his head with it, Nichiren wrote later. The particular scroll of the sutra was section five, which contained the thirteenth chapter. Nichiren was struck with awe when he realized that for his faith intolerant men assaulted him with a scroll that contained the very chapter describing the persecution a votary of the Lotus Sutra was expected to endure. Nichiren's reaction to the experience was ambivalent; although mortified by the outrage, it was, he recalled several years later, also satisfying for him.

Nichiren was arrested ostensibly for exile to Sado, but the Hojos had actually intended to execute him. In the early hours of the day after his arrest, Nichiren was taken to a place called Tatsunokuchi in Kamakura. But just as a soldier made ready to swing down his sword to behead him, a "ball of light like that of the moon flew from the direction of Enoshima, blinding the executioner, who, frightened, fell down to the ground."[6] Nichiren escaped death because of this famous "miracle" at Tatsunokuchi, and after nearly a month's detention he was escorted to Sado, where he was kept for two and a half years.

---

[6] Popular legend has it that the ball of light broke the sword in half, thus saving Nichiren's life. Historians prefer to think that it was lightning that struck the sword of the executioner and frightened him.

Nichiren's life on the desolate island of Sado in the Sea of Japan profoundly influenced the development of his thought and religious conviction. With time to cogitate—in particular, about the reason for his subjection to continual hardships—he produced two important works: *Kaimokusho* and *Kanjin no Honzonsho* (also known as *Kanjinhonzonsho*). In *Kaimokusho* (Treatise on Eye-Opening), Nichiren compared the various religions and philosophical systems to reach what he believed was the ultimate truth and discussed it in detail in *Kanjin no Honzonsho.*[7] This document gives an elaborate exposition of Nichiren's own cosmology and doctrinal system, based on the assumed supremacy of the Lotus Sutra in the age of *mappo*.

Throughout these and other writings Nichiren produced during his exile on Sado, he was searching for reasons for the difficulties he encountered. The reasons he found may be summarized as 1) his personal guilt or responsibility in a previous incarnation, 2) the guardian deities' abandonment of the country, 3) the fact that the human world, being finite and imperfect, allows hardships to be imposed on an individual such as Nichiren, and 4) hardship is the lot of a bodhisattva who chooses to live in a finite and foul age so as to give expression to the ultimate truth, like a lotus flower blooming out of mud.

To Nichiren, the most important reason was the fourth. It seems to have either convinced or nearly convinced him that he was a bodhisattva destined to spread the gospel of the Lotus Sutra. He found reassurance for his assumption in Chapters 10 through 22 of the sutra.

In 1274, Nichiren was allowed to return to Kamakura. He arrived on March 26, after a twenty-day journey from Sado. Although his followers must have expected their teacher to resume activities in Kamakura, Nichiren preferred not to. On May 12, he left for the deep woods of Minobu in today's Yamanashi Prefecture. The year 1274 is another significant milestone in his career. On April 8, prior to Nichiren's depar-

---

[7] *Kanjin no Honzonsho* is the abbreviated form of *Nyorai Metsugo Go no Gohyakusai ni Hajimu Kanjin no Honzonsho,* which Soka Gakkai translates as *Writings on the Supreme Object of Worship in the True Buddhism Originated in the Fifth Millennium After the Death of Sakyamuni.* A free translation of *Kanjin no Honzonsho* is *Treatise on the Attainment of Buddhahood in the Era of Mappo.*

ture for Minobu, a high-ranking samurai in the shogunate government asked him when the Mongols would attack Japan. Nichiren replied that it would be "not beyond the end of this year."

"Although the sutra does not say exactly when," he said, "Heaven seems to be furious [over the failure of the government to adopt the correct religion]." The prediction was borne out in October that year when the Mongols came to Kyushu.

But why did Nichiren leave Kamakura, the *de facto* capital of Japan, to live as a recluse in the woods of the province of Kai? When asked about the time of Mongols' attack, Nichiren added that the shogunate must not ask priests of the Shingon sect to pray for the nation's safety, because to do so would be "a major calamity for the land. . . . If you ask Shingon priests to offer prayer to drive back the invaders, this country will be truly ruined," he told the shogunate official.

The statement reflects Nichiren's unswerving conviction of the exclusive truth of his own religious dogma. To Nichiren, the eternal Buddha was the only personality whom all sects must acknowledge as supreme. Amidabutsu (Amitabha), the Buddha worshiped by followers of the Jodo sect, for instance, symbolized the infinite light emanating from the eternal Buddha—not the Buddha himself. Chih-i, the founder of the T'ien-t'ai sect of China, had alluded to all other Buddhas as mere reflections in ponds of the image of the moon, which is the only truth. Nichiren (whose doctrine had its basis in the Tendai theology) likewise described those who "worshiped the other Buddhas" as failing to know the true Buddha, whom all must acknowledge.

Despite Nichiren's warning, the shogunate asked a high priest of a Shingon temple to offer a prayer for rain on April 10. It did rain on the following day, April 11, but April 12 brought a disastrous storm that cost many lives and destroyed many homes. Nichiren attributed this to the prayer by the wrong priest. This storm is believed to have been a major disaster of 1274, for a chronicle describing the Hojo era notes for that year two principal calamities—the damage caused by the storm of April 12 and the Mongols' landing on the island of Tsushima off Kyushu on October 5.

The Mongol invasion prompted the shogunate and the

imperial court to ask priests of important temples of various sects to offer prayers for the repulse of the invaders. Nichiren objected to this, not because he did not approve of prayer as such but because he believed that all sects must be subordinated to the supreme canon of the Lotus Sutra.

Nichiren's injunctions were again ignored, and he came to despair of the salvation of the secular society in which he lived. Later, he wrote that he had left Kamakura following the old maxim, "If you admonish the government three times and it does not heed your advice, then you must go into the woods." He chose Minobu as a refuge from the mundane world because the area belonged to Hagiri Sanenaga, an influential follower of Nichiren, who was a local administrator for the Hojos.

At Minobu, Nichiren further refined his doctrine of Buddhism, which he imparted to his followers. His priestly disciples conducted evangelism in the Kanto region (eastern Japan) and areas closer to Minobu. The stepped-up activities, however, increased both opposition to Nichirenism and persecution of his followers. A typical development was the martyrdom known as the *honan* ("hardship suffered by a votary") of Atsuhara, a place in today's Yoshihara, Shizuoka Prefecture.

In 1279, twenty peasants who had been converted to Nichirenism by Nikko, the highest disciple of Nichiren, were arrested and detained at Kamakura mainly in response to the jealous urging of Tendai priests. Because they refused to renounce their faith, they were jailed for six months before three of them were beheaded and the rest banished from the area. Nichiren was deeply impressed by the martyrdom and stressed in a letter the importance of dying for the truth and for love of one's fellow men.

Some of his followers, including a few close disciples, gave way under oppression. Nichiren was stern with such men who renounced their faith. Yet he also sympathized with them because he knew better than anyone else, from personal experience, how difficult it was to suffer persecution—particularly for lay adherents with families. He expressed these feelings eloquently in his personal letters that are still preserved.

While Nichiren relished the secluded, otherworldly life at

Minobu, it nevertheless cost him his health. Weakened by the penetrating cold of the mountains, he began to suffer chronic diarrhea toward the end of 1278. In a letter written in mid-1279, he spoke of "a disease which reduced my weight," and said that he "suffered so much that I find it difficult to write." A medicine prepared by a follower with some medical knowledge brought temporary relief. The winter of 1279, however, was particularly cold at Minobu, and he had a relapse. Because of the excessive cold, which he likened to the "hell of cold" mentioned in the sutras, he failed to improve. He predicted in a letter of May 26, 1281, that he would not live much longer—not more than one or two years beyond the end of that year.

In December he could scarcely eat because of the debilitating illness and old age. In September 1282, he decided to treat his ailment at a hot spring in the province of Hitachi (today's Ibaraki Prefecture). Nichiren left Minobu on a horse offered by Hagiri, accompanied by attendants. On September 18, he arrived at Ikegami (in the present-day Ota Ward of Tokyo) for a stopover. His last letter, addressed to Hagiri and thanking him for his kindnesses, was dictated to his pupil Nikko. By then Nichiren was so weak that he could not even sign the letter, much less resume the journey to Hitachi. Nichiren died on October 13, and in accordance with his will his ashes were buried at Minobu.

NICHIREN'S SUCCESSORS

When he died, Nichiren's disciples numbered only about 260. One authority estimates that he had perhaps 65 clerical disciples and 160-odd lay adherents.[8]

In the centuries after his death, his following splintered over different interpretations of his doctrine, thus giving rise to many schools and subsects of what may be generally called the Nichiren sect.

Five days before his death, on October 8, 1282, Nichiren summoned to his bedside his six most important pupils and

---

[8] Tamura, Yoshiro: *Yogensha no Bukkyo: Rissho Ankoku Ron* (The Buddhism of a Prophet: *Rissho Ankoku Ron*), Chikuma Shobo, Tokyo, 1967, p. 204.

designated them as his official disciples. Known as the Roku Roso (Six Senior Priests), they were Nichiji (1250–?), Nitcho (1252–1317), Niko (1253–1314), Nikko (1246–1333), Nichiro (1245–1320), and Nissho (1221?–1323). Nichiren bequeathed his teachings to Nikko, the closest of his disciples, who had served often as his secretary. Nikko had followed Nichiren to Sado and stayed with him for two and a half years, sharing with his master all the trials and sufferings of exile.

Born in 1246 at Kajikasawa in the province of Kai (today's Yamanashi Prefecture), Nikko began to study the Tendai doctrine of Buddhism at the age of twelve at Shinjuku-in temple at Kambara, in today's Shizuoka Prefecture. When Nichiren went to Jisso-ji to study the sutras, Nikko became his pupil and from that time remained with Nichiren. Nikko's own evangelizing won many of the lay adherents who played a prominent role in Nichiren's life. Hagiri of Minobu was one; another was Nanjo Tokimitsu, who later helped Nikko found the new temple, Taiseki-ji, at Fuji. Nikko also converted the famous martyrs of Atsuhara described above. Their martyrdom deeply shocked Nikko while also intensifying his religious convictions and his doctrinal studies. At the same time, it strengthened the teacher-pupil bond between Nichiren and Nikko. It was natural that Nichiren should treat Nikko as his most senior pupil, since his merits outshone those of all the others.

After Nichiren's death, eighteen of his followers—including the Six Senior Priests—agreed to serve, in turns of one month each, as keepers of their master's grave at Minobu. The twelve priests other than the Six were chosen from the local Minobu area. Of the twelve, nine were Nikko's own pupils.

The system of rotation, however, did not work out well, partly because three of the Six Senior Priests, whose bases of operation were in the distant Kanto region, found the task inconvenient. Nor was Minobu, a remote corner in the woods, an important center for further evangelism. Apparently, the system of rotation was observed for only a short period. Since missionary work was their first duty, the Senior Priests returned to their respective regions.

After the first annual memorial service for Nichiren, Nikko settled at Kuon-ji temple at Minobu as head priest. Nissho and Nichiro lived in Kamakura and carried on their conversion programs in the provinces of Musashi (today's Tokyo) and Sagami (Kanagawa). Niko did likewise in Kazusa (Ibaraki and northern Chiba) and Nitcho in Shimo-osa (southern Chiba). The areas around Minobu (Yamanashi) and much of Shizuoka, including the Izu Peninsula, were territories covered by Nikko and his own disciples, such as Nichiji. Nichiji, however, later left his teacher and sided with Nissho and Nichiro in Kamakura. In 1294, Nichiji started on a long evangelical journey to Hokkaido, the Maritime Province of Siberia, Hopeh Province of China, and even to Mongolia. He is believed to have died somewhere on the Asiatic continent.

The lack of solidarity among the Six Senior Priests was evident only a year after Nichiren's death. Only Nikko and his own disciples attended the service held at Minobu on the first anniversary of Nichiren's death. The five others held their own rites at Ikegami, where Nichiren had died. Nor did they attend the second anniversary service at Kuon-ji temple. Nikko considered this as a sign of diminishing loyalty to the master. Then Nissho, who was originally a Tendai priest, reverted to the old school, and Nichiro, Niko, and Nitcho followed suit. Nikko, at Minobu, was understandably critical, and the breach between him and the five others widened.

Hagiri, the local administrator for the shogunate at Minobu, later became friendly with the five other priests, despite the fact that Nikko had originally converted him. Furthermore, to Nikko's horror, Hagiri committed the worst sin for a Nichirenite: he paid homage to a Shinto shrine and made offerings to temples of other sects in the area under his jurisdiction. A puritan in the interpretation and practice of Nichiren's teachings, Nikko could not tolerate Hagiri's acts of apostasy. But when admonished, Hagiri dared to defy Nikko. This compelled Nikko to leave Minobu, because a Buddhist priest of that time could not maintain a temple and its parish without the support of the local administrative official.

Nikko left Kuon-ji in December 1288 and went to live at the foot of Mount Fuji, where he founded Taiseki-ji temple in 1290 with the assistance of the local administrator Nanjo Tokimitsu. The temple was named Taiseki-ji (Big Rock Temple) because the locality was known as Oishigahara (Big Rock Plain), after a large rock which today stands in the grounds of Taiseki-ji.

The founding of Taiseki-ji only eight years after Nichiren's death signified that the religious legacy of Nichiren was already split among his pupils. In 1298—less than eight years later—Nikko built another temple, the Hommon-ji, at Omosu, not far from Taiseki-ji. Here he opened a sectarian school for vigorous doctrinal training. Nikko lived at Hommon-ji until his death in 1333 at the age of eighty-seven.

Obviously a priest of considerable ability and influence, Nikko laid the basis for the elaborate doctrinal system of today's Nichiren Shoshu, with commentaries on and paraphrases of his master's thought and theory. Nikko's primary work—his commentaries on and exegeses of Nichiren's doctrine, *Ongi Kuden*—is a cornerstone of Nichiren Shoshu theology. It is one of the essential readings for members of Soka Gakkai today.

Like his master, Nikko designated six of his top pupils as the Six Senior Priests, to which he later added a further six. These followers zealously carried out their mission to spread the teachings of Nichiren throughout Japan. They were undoubtedly stimulated by its rivalry with the Minobu-temple Nichirenites and by their conviction that they themselves were the only true heirs to Nichiren's canon.

The school of faith which Nikko began was known as Fuji Monryu, after its place of origin, or as Nikko Monryu, after the founder.[9] But this sect too was racked by continual doctrinal disputes and personal rivalries which caused more splits. Each of the subsects then proclaimed itself the only orthodox successor to Nikko. Chief among them were the orders at Taiseki-ji and Hommon-ji temples. Because Taiseki-ji was the first temple Nikko founded, it claimed to be the headquarters of all Nichiren temples. Hommon-ji based its assertion of authority on the fact that Nikko lived there far longer than at Taiseki-ji and that he named it Hommon-ji (Temple of True Teaching), which implied that he himself considered it the chief temple of his order.

---

[9] *Monryu* literally means "gate and stream," "gate" being the traditional Buddhist expression for the Buddha's teaching and "stream" meaning a school of thought or, as used in later eras, of any of the traditional arts or skills.

After the latter part of the sixteenth century, however, all the subbranches of Nikko Monryu, except the one at Taiseki-ji, were reconciled, attaining unity of a sort under the title of Nikko Monryu. The Taiseki-ji subsect remained an independent and isolated minority group. In 1912, it renamed itself Nichiren Shoshu to indicate its total independence of the Nichiren sect at Minobu and of other subsects of Nikko Monryu.

The Basis of the Claim of Orthodoxy

Nichiren Shoshu bases its claim of orthodoxy on two chief sources: 1) the two documents in which Nichiren bequeathed his teachings to Nikko and 2) the Daigohonzon, the sacred tablet that substantiates the succession and that Nichiren Shoshu claims is the testament left by Nichiren for mankind.

In Buddhist tradition a key determinant of doctrinal succession is *kechimyaku sojo* (literally, "inheritance of blood")—that is, bequest of a Buddhist canon by a master to the single, chosen disciple. Sakyamuni the Buddha, for instance, is believed to have handed down his teachings to Maha-Kasyapa, who in turn bequeathed them to Ananda.

One of the documents on which Nichiren Shoshu bases its claim that Nikko was Nichiren's chosen disciple is a short statement, known as *Minobu Sojosho,* written by Nichiren in September 1282, shortly before he left Minobu on his last journey. The second is called *Ikegami Sojosho,* written on the day Nichiren died at Ikegami, which states that he appointed Nikko as high priest of Kuon-ji at Minobu. Although the originals of these two papers were lost some time after 1540, their copies are kept at Taiseki-ji. However, the rival Nichiren sect, not surprisingly, claims that these documents are forged.

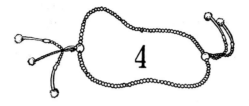

The Doctrine
of Nichiren Shoshu

Ichinen Sanzen

One of the cardinal elements of Nichiren's teachings is the theory of *ichinen sanzen,* based on the system of the same name expounded by Chih-i, founder[1] of China's T'ien-t'ai sect of Buddhism, in his classic work *Mo-ho Chih-kuan* (in Japanese, *Maka Shikan*). *Ichinen sanzen* (in Chinese, *i-nen-san-chien*)—literally, "one thought three thousand"—means that the human mind at any moment incorporates the universe in its three thousand aspects.

The figure three thousand is arrived at in the following way. The human mind is said to be in one of the *jikkai* (ten states) at any particular moment. The ten states are 1) *jigoku* (hell): the state of suffering from any cause; 2) *gaki* (craving): the state of being dominated by desire; 3) *chikusho* (animality): the state of shortsightedly failing to see the eternal fundamentals underlying the here and now; 4) *shura* (anger): the state of being angry and contentious; 5) *nin* (tranquility): the state of being peaceful—neither positively happy nor unhappy; 6) *ten* (rapture): the state of being joyful, as when one's wish has been fulfilled; 7) *shomon* (intellectual pleasure): the state of pleasure derived from learning; 8) *engaku* (learning the law): the state of being ecstatic over having learned a

---

[1] Chih-i may also be regarded as the third-generation master of the T'ien-t'ai sect of Buddhism when Hui-wen and Hui-su are considered his predecessors.

45

truth; 9) *bosatsu* (bodhisattva) : the state of working for others and the community with courage, wisdom, mercy, and other virtues; 10) *butsu* (Buddhahood) : the state of being aware of the true meaning of life that is eternal and of living a life that is wholesome—mentally, physically, and financially.

According to *ichinen sanzen*, the human mind at any moment is in one of these ten conditions, ranging from hell to Buddhahood. In each state of mind, however, are found the same ten, bringing to one hundred the total number of states of mind.

The state of mind is also grasped in *junyoze* or ten *nyoze*. The word *nyoze*, which is of Chinese origin, seems to have no precise counterpart in a Western language, and the explanations of the ten *nyoze* offered by Soka Gakkai in its publications make the concept of *nyoze* appear to be one of the most esoteric elements of Nichiren Shoshu theology.

A non-Soka Gakkai source translates *junyoze* into English as "ten factors of existence,"[2] while Soka Gakkai translates it as "ten aspects of life." The "ten aspects" are listed as "appearance, nature, entity, power, action, cause, relationship, effect, reward, and consistency from beginning to end."[3]

Soka Gakkai's official commentary on Nichiren Shoshu theology does not seem to clarify the esoteric concepts for the uninitiated. It defines the *junyoze* as follows: 1) *nyozeso* is the external appearance, material things, the corporal body; 2) *nyozesho* is inner qualities such as the spirit, mind, and wisdom; 3) *nyozetai* is life; 4) *nyozeriki* is inherent strength; 5) *nyozesa* is the function of that strength; 6) *nyozein* is that function which serves as the cause of something for life itself; 7) *nyoze-en* and 8) *nyozeka* are the consequences of *nyozein;* 9) *nyozeho* is the reward one finds in the consequence of a cause; and 10) *nyoze-hommatsukukyoto* (also *nyoze-hommakkukyoto*) is the consistency found throughout the nine "aspects of life."[4]

---

[2] *Japanese-English Buddhist Dictionary*, Daito Shuppansha, Tokyo, 1965.

[3] *Seikyo Times*, February 1968, p. 67.

[4] Soka Gakkai Kyogakubu (Study Department, Soka Gakkai) : *Nichiren Shoshu Kyogaku Kaisetsu* (Commentaries on Nichiren Shoshu Doctrine), Tokyo, 1963, pp. 141–43.

The one hundred states of the mind multiplied by ten produce one thousand. This is further multiplied by three, to take account of the *sanseken* (three categories) of human life, namely *go-on seken, shujo seken,* and *kokudo seken. Go-on seken* is the individual's physical and mental activities, classified as *shiki* (corporal body), *ju* (sensory perception), *so* (retention of what has been received), *gyo* (action stimulated by what has been retained), and *shiki* (the mind responsible for *ju, so,* and *gyo*).[5] *Shujo seken* is the relationship between the individual and other members of his community; *kokudo seken* is the environment in which an individual personality exists.[6] It is thus that the figure three thousand is derived.

The theory of *ichinen sanzen,* as elaborated by Chih-i, is supposed to be a comprehensive scheme of human life and its relationship with the universe. Nichiren, however, did not regard it as absolutely valid, describing it as *ri no ichinen sanzen,* meaning "*ichinen sanzen* in theory," as against his own version, which he called *ji no ichinen sanzen*—"*ichinen sanzen* in practice."

Chih-i's *ichinen sanzen* was simply an objective, rational understanding of the nature of man and the universe which did not actively involve the individual. Nichiren's version, on the other hand, entailed the participation of the individual who sought understanding: a pragmatic rather than theoretical approach. To Nichiren the theory of intellectual attainment that Chih-i propounded did not help man attain the ultimate goal of Buddhahood, because it did not tell him what he must do to reach this state.

What one must do, according to Nichiren, was to commit himself to the Lotus Sutra, with which he identified his own version of *ichinen sanzen.* In one of his writings he said that the

---

[5] *Japanese-English Buddhist Dictionary,* Tokyo, 1965, translates *go-on* (also *go-un;* in Sanskrit, *panca skandha*) as "the five aggregates" and offers the following definition: "All physical, mental, and other elements in this phenomenal world *(samskara-dharma)* are classified into five kinds of aggregates in Buddhist philosophy." The five aggregates are given as 1) *shikiun:* a generic term for all forms of matter; 2) *ju-un:* perception; 3) *soun:* mental conception and ideas; 4) *gyoun:* volition; and 5) *shikiun:* consciousness of mind. *Go-on seken* is defined as "the five *skandhas* that constitute every being."

[6] Soka Gakkai's translation of *sanseken's* components is *go-on seken:* elements; *shujo seken:* life; and *kokudo seken:* place. *The Seikyo Times,* February 1968, p. 68.

Daigohonzon, the "great mandala" he produced for mankind, was the actual embodiment of his theory of *ichinen sanzen.*

GOKO: THE FIVE PRINCIPLES

Another key element of Nichiren's doctrine is the *goko* (five principles), the criteria Nichiren employed to compare various religions and assert the supremacy of his own. The five principles are 1) *kyo:* canon; 2) *ki:* the readiness of people to accept the canon; 3) *ji:* time or timing; 4) *koku:* country; and 5) *kyoho rufu no sengo:* the sequence in which religious teaching may be spread.

What Nichiren meant was that, first, it was important to judge which of the numerous sutras preached by the Buddha was supreme. The answer, needless to say, was the Lotus Sutra. Yet even this supreme sutra could not be taught without regard to the readiness of the people for it—hence the second criterion. According to Nichiren, people in his age were ready to be taught the sutra (i.e., the "Nam-myoho Renge-kyo").

The third criterion was the timing of preaching: in what kind of era to preach what sutra. Nichiren was convinced that in the age of *mappo* only the Lotus Sutra was to be preached. Fourthly, a religion must be chosen with regard to the country concerned, and in Japan, Nichiren believed, Mahayana Buddhism and the Lotus Sutra in particular must be propagated. Lastly, he held that anyone trying to spread a religion in a country must know what kind of religion prevailed there before. In a country where Buddhism had not previously been introduced, Hinayana Buddhism might be spread, he thought. But in the case of Japan, the only faith to be established should be that of the Lotus Sutra.

Thus this theory—that of the *goko*—also affirms Nichiren's ultimate belief in the Lotus Sutra as the absolute and supreme canon of Buddhism.

SANSHO: THE THREE PROOFS

Still another criterion to confirm the relative superiority of religions, according to Nichiren Shoshu theology, is *sansho,* the three proofs, namely the proofs by written language, by logic, and by reality.

By the proof by written language *(monsho)* is meant documentary proof of the superiority of a religion. To put it in the reverse way, it is possible to assess the value of a religious teaching by assessing the literary material on which it is based, such as historical records and sutras. According to this criterion, one religion that fails to qualify as a good religion is Zen Buddhism, because its doctrine rejects the use of written language. For this reason, Nichiren classified Zen as an evil religion.

The proof by logic *(risho)* is explained by Nichiren himself, who said: "Buddhism is a logic, which means that a good religion must be logically coherent and valid." A superior religion must be so logical that it convinces people in all ages and in all parts of the world—that is, it must have universal validity, according to the theory of the three proofs.

Thirdly, the superiority of a religion must be proven by reality. Nichiren considered this *gensho* (proof by reality) the most important of the three proofs, because no matter how superior a religious doctrine may be, it is worthless unless its superiority is borne out by reality—for example, by the fact that people who are committed to it are happy.

Goju no Sotai: The Five Comparisons

The five comparisons consist of five pairs of the superior and inferior and show the ultimate superiority of Nichiren Shoshu over all other forms of Buddhism as well as other religions.

The first, called *naige sotai,* is the comparison of the "in" with the "out"—that is, Buddhism with non-Buddhist religions, such as Christianity, Hinduism, or Islam. Soka Gakkai documents on Nichiren Shoshu theology state that Buddhism is superior to other religions because, based on the law of cause and effect, it is scientific while other religions are unscientific. They "totally ignore the law of cause and effect." Christian theology, for instance, is said to be "a highly unscientific dogma" because it holds as truth such theories as those of the

Creation, the Immaculate Conception, and the Resurrection.[7]

The second comparison, *daisho sotai*, is that between Mahayana Buddhism and Hinayana Buddhism, of which the former is held superior.

The third, *gonjitsu sotai*, is the comparison between false Mahayana Buddhism and true Mahayana Buddhism. By the former is meant such other Japanese Buddhist sects as Nembutsu, Shingon, and Zen, while the latter means Nichiren Shoshu.

Honjaku sotai, the fourth comparison, is the comparison of *hommon* (true teaching) with *shakumon* (provisional teaching), or "substance" with its "shadow." By the former are meant the teachings found in the first fourteen chapters of the twenty-eight-chapter Lotus Sutra while the latter refers to the remaining fourteen chapters. According to Nichiren Shoshu theology, the Buddha's teachings found in the first half of the Lotus Sutra constitute his "theoretical canon," which corresponds to *ri no ichinen sanzen* (*ichinen sanzen* in theory) while the latter half represents the substance of the teachings, comprising his cosmology based on the theory of eternal life. This corresponds to *ji no ichinen sanzen* (*ichinen sanzen* in practice). Soka Gakkai documents compare the two components of the Lotus Sutra to blueprints and the house built on the basis of the blueprints, respectively, and hold the latter superior to the former.[8]

The fifth comparison, called *shudatsu sotai*, is the comparison between Sakyamuni's Buddhism and Nichiren's Buddhism. The *shu* of *shudatsu* stands for *geshu*, which means sowing— sowing the seed of attaining Buddhahood. *Datsu*, on the other hand, represents *datchaku* and means harvesting as a result of sowing—that is, attaining Buddhahood. According to Nichiren Shoshu, "Buddhism of *datchaku*" is the Buddhism of Sakyamuni the Buddha, which is ineffective in the age of *mappo*, while "Buddhism of *geshu*" is Nichiren's Buddhism, which in the age of *mappo* enables a common man to attain Buddhahood instantly if only he commits himself to the Lotus Sutra. Of the two, the latter is held superior.

[7] Soka Gakkai Kyogakubu, *op. cit.*, p. 115.
[8] *Ibid.*, pp. 116–17.

THE THREE GREAT SECRET LAWS

Probably the most important component of the doctrine developed by Nichiren is the *sandai hiho:* the "three great secret laws" to which he reduced his Buddhism. Although the term *hiho* consists of two Chinese characters which today stand for "secret" and "law," as a Buddhist term it means "profound theory or law." *Sandai hiho,* then, signifies simply "three extremely important things." According to Nichiren, these were the *honzon:* the sacred object of worship; the *daimoku:* the title of the sutra; and the *kaidan:* the ordination platform. Each of these terms was modified by the adjective *hommon no,* meaning "of the true teaching."

The interpretation of these three terms has been a basic point of disagreement between Nichiren Shoshu and other Nichiren sects. According to the latter, *honzon* is the eternal Buddha who manifested himself in the form of the historical Buddha, while *daimoku* is the title of the Lotus Sutra, read in Japanese as *Myoho Renge-kyo. Kaidan,* the ordination platform (which Nichiren referred to with no precise definition), has been given various interpretations. They range from a structure—an actual platform—to an abstract concept: the condition in which every individual believes in the Lotus Sutra, or the state of the world when the teachings of Nichiren universally prevail.

The Nichiren Shoshu interpretations of the "three great secret laws" differ radically from those of the other sects. *Honzon,* for instance, is the mandala, a graphic symbol of the universe, which originated in ancient India. Introduced into Buddhism during the early centuries, the traditional Buddhist mandala symbolized deities and bodhisattvas in a graphic arrangement. It held an important position in the Shingon and Tendai sects of Buddhism in Japan.

Nichiren, trained initially in Tendai theology, created a new type of mandala. It had the sacred phrase "Nam-myoho Renge-kyo"[9] (Devotion to the Lotus Sutra), written vertically

---

[9] Nichiren Shoshu makes a meticulous distinction regarding the pronunciation of the sacred phrase. It is recited as "Nam-myoho Renge-kyo," whereas other Nichiren sects pronounce it "Namu Myoho Renge-kyo."

in the center, around which were arranged names of various deities as if to safeguard the seven-ideograph phrase. It symbolizes the absolute superiority of the Lotus Sutra over other religions and sects, which are represented by deities that include Shinto gods as well as Buddhist supernatural beings.

Nichiren inscribed many mandalas of this kind, which he gave his disciples and followers. Since they were entitled to these mandalas only while they lived, the mandalas were returned to Taiseki-ji after their deaths. This accounts for the surprising number of extant handwritten tablets by Nichiren.

These *honzon*, or mandalas, given to individuals, were written on pieces of paper which were made into scrolls and hung in the altars at the recipients' homes. The mandala regarded as one of the "three great secret laws" of Nichiren Shoshu, however, is a large wooden tablet on which the sacred letters are carved. It is kept in the *hoanden* (sanctuary) of Taiseki-ji temple and is known as the Daigohonzon ("great object of worship").

According to Soka Gakkai, *hommon no daimoku* means the pious practice of chanting "Nam-myoho Renge-kyo" while believing in the *hommon no honzon*, the sacred tablet at Taiseki-ji. That is, Soka Gakkai gives the term *daimoku* a significance beyond its literal meaning, which is "the title of a sutra." The seven-character phrase "Nam-myoho Renge-kyo" is the name of a sutra preceded by the Sanskrit term *nam*, meaning "devotion." To Soka Gakkai, this phrase itself is more important than the whole of the sutra. Hence the great importance attached to the practice of chanting the phrase hundreds, thousands, and tens of thousands of times a day.

The interpretation of the third "great secret law," *kaidan*, is one of the most controversial features of Soka Gakkai and Nichiren Shoshu. According to Nichiren Shoshu, there are two kinds of *kaidan* to be built. One is a *gi no kaidan* (a *kaidan* in meaning), which can be any place as long as a *honzon* is worshiped. So the altar at the home of a Nichiren Shoshu adherent, where a *honzon* is kept and the recipient of the *honzon* pays homage to it, would be a *gi no kaidan*. The other is a *ji no kaidan* (a *kaidan* in reality), which, according to Soka Gakkai literature, means the ordination platform to be erected

A New Force in Religion

10. *Daikyakuden (Grand Reception Hall) at Taiseki-ji. The building, designed by Kimio Yokoyama and completed in 1964, was donated to Taiseki-ji by Soka Gakkai. Its main worship hall seats 5,000 persons.*

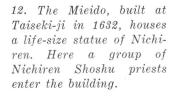

11. *The Shimonobo, now part of the grand complex of Taiseki-ji, was the private temple of the layman Nanjo Tokimitsu, who assisted Nichiren's disciple Nikko in founding Taiseki-ji in 1290. Nikko stayed in the Shimonobo while Taiseki-ji was being built.*

12. *The Mieido, built at Taiseki-ji in 1632, houses a life-size statue of Nichiren. Here a group of Nichiren Shoshu priests enter the building.*

13. *Aerial view of Taiseki-ji, with Mount Fuji in the background.*

14. *The Mutsubo (Six-Compartment Temple) at Taiseki-ji. This temple, rebuilt in 1965, follows the design of the original, built in the thirteenth century by Nikko, founder of Taiseki-ji.*

15. *A ritual procession at Taiseki-ji heads for the Mieido,
where a statue of Nichiren is enshrined.*

16. In the presence of priests and laymen, sacred treasures, including mandalas written by Nichiren, are displayed at Taiseki-ji. President Ikeda of Soka Gakkai (left rear), is seen wearing a chief laymen's robe.

17. One of the annual rites at Taiseki-ji is the Cup Ceremony, in which priests drink sakè in praise of Nichiren.

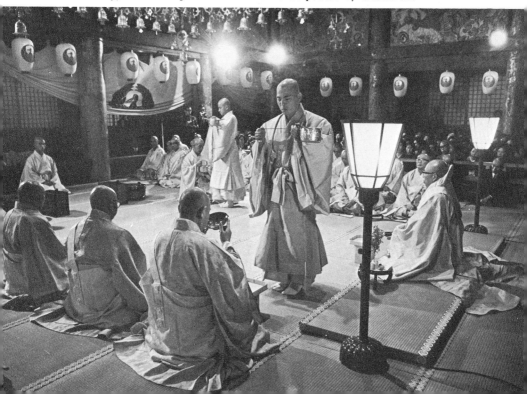

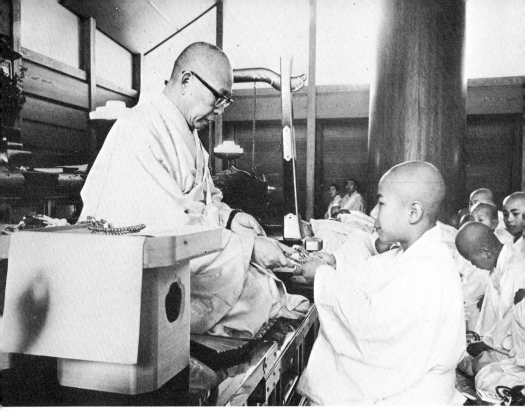

18. *A newly tonsured boy priest at Taiseki-ji receives a rosary and a book of sutras from High Priest Nittatsu during an ordination ceremony.*

19. *English is one of the courses offered for Nichiren Shoshu priests attending summer seminars at Taiseki-ji.*

20. *The steamer* Fuji *is one of two ships chartered by Soka Gakkai on a semipermanent basis to transport pilgrims from Shikoku and Kyushu to the port nearest to Taiseki-ji.*

21. *The Myoho-ji temple at Etiwanda, near Los Angeles, was opened for American members of Soka Gakkai (known as Nichiren Shoshu in the United States) in May 1967.*

22. *New Year's service at Soka Gakkai's Myoho-ji temple in Etiwanda, California.*

23. *A family of Soka Gakkai members conducts morning prayers before the* gohonzon.

upon the completion of *kosen rufu* (propagation of the teachings of Nichiren throughout the world). The term *kaidan* in this context, however, is not to be interpreted literally; it means a large hall of worship where the entire nation or world can congregate to worship.

This theory is based on Nichiren's *Sandai Hihosho*, in which he said: "The *kaidan* is to be erected at a scenic spot which should resemble Grdhrakuta,[10] with a *chokusen* (imperial decree) and a *migyosho* (shogunate order), after Buddhism and government become united and when the ruler and his subjects all acquire the three secret laws of the true teaching and are ready to re-create, in the foul age of *mappo*, the past achievements of Utokuo and Kakutoku Biku.[11] We must only wait for such a day."

Nichiren Shoshu claims that in the *Minobu Sojosho*, the statement in which Nichiren bequeathed his canon to Nikko, Nichiren willed that "the *kaidan* of the *hommon* temple should be erected at Mount Fuji."

According to Nichiren Shoshu and Soka Gakkai, the erection of the *kaidan* is the only task left unfinished by Nichiren—the task which his spiritual heirs, such as members of Soka Gakkai, are now endeavoring to accomplish.

NICHIREN'S IDENTITY

Aside from the complex doctrinal system that Nichiren

[10] Grdhrakuta is a mountain in Bengal, India, where the Buddha is believed to have preached the teachings of the Lotus Sutra. In Japanese Buddhist literature, the peak is known as Gishakussen or Ryojusen. The former is the Japanese adaptation of the Chinese phonetic transcription of "Grdhrakuta," and the latter is a descriptive name, meaning literally "Holy Eagle Mountain." The "eagle" here is more correctly the vulture, because vultures were numerous near the mountain, feeding on the corpses abandoned nearby. Thus English writers refer to the mountain as the Vulture Peak. To believers in the Lotus Sutra, however, the Vulture Peak is a sacred symbol of the teachings of the Buddha. Nichiren Shoshu and Soka Gakkai liken Taiseki-ji to this symbolic mountain.

[11] According to the Nehan-gyo (also Daihatsu Nehan-gyo; in Sanskrit, Mahaparinibbanasuttanta), a sutra translated into Chinese during the fourth century, a ruler named Utokuo, in an allegorical episode in the life of the eternal Buddha, battled against enemies of his faith in order to safeguard a monk named Kakutoku Biku who was defending the "right law." The king suffered injuries all over his body and was about to die. The monk praised him for his good deed, and the king died a happy man.

expounded, the most important question to his followers and
to any one attempting to understand the doctrine of Nichiren
Shoshu is Nichiren's own view of himself in relation to the
Buddha. For this is a crucial issue over which Nichiren Shoshu
and other Nichiren sects disagree.

Nichiren's words, like the words of the sutra, are often
ambiguous, which partly accounts for the doctrinal disputes
among his followers. Nevertheless, his basic premises seem
clear. Having studied the Lotus Sutra, Nichiren came to believe
that the age of *mappo* had indeed begun in the first part of
the eleventh century. In this sad eon, according to the sutra,
the teaching of the Buddha would be ineffectual in saving man.
What the Buddha preached must be preached anew by bodhisattvas, pupils, and emissaries of the Buddha. Nichiren
apparently came very close to identifying himself with—or
actually believed himself to be—Jogyo Bosatsu (Visistacaritra
Bodhisattva), the leader of the bodhisattvas who were to
appear in the age of *mappo*, as prophesied in the fifteenth
chapter of the Lotus Sutra, entitled "Jujiyujuppon."

The most commonly accepted view is that Nichiren thought
he was Jogyo Bosatsu. This is based on his repeated references
to this particular chapter of the sutra and the conviction with
which he pursued his mission of salvation. There are also many
passages which suggest that Nichiren all but identified himself
with that particular bodhisattva. In an essay he wrote at the
age of fifty, for instance, he says. "Having been born in this
corrupt and depraved age of *mappo*, I have endured attacks
by formidable enemies while reciting 'Nam-myoho Renge-kyo.'
How can I not be an emissary of the Buddha?" About the same
time, he wrote to Shijo Kingo, one of his lay followers: "A
person who recites the Lotus Sutra and tells others about it
is a messenger of the Buddha. Though I, Nichiren, am of
humble origin, I came to this land with the Buddha's
credentials."

At the age of fifty-one, Nichiren wrote that he was "the
only herald of the bodhisattvas who arose from the earth,"
referring to a passage in the fifteenth chapter of the sutra,
and that he might be "counted as one of them. If so, why
should Nichiren's disciples and lay adherents not be also
kin of the bodhisattvas?"

In *Senjisho*, a treatise Nichiren wrote at Minobu when he was fifty-three, he says: "There is no doubt that I, Nichiren, am the foremost practitioner of the Lotus Sutra in Japan."

These remarks are open to various interpretations, both literal and figurative, but it is not surprising that his followers should identify him with Jogyo Bosatsu, thereby deifying him and building up a cult of individual worship.

Despite all this, Nichiren did not anywhere state outright that he was Jogyo Bosatsu. At least one authority maintains that Nichiren regarded himself neither as Jogyo Bosatsu nor as an emissary of the Buddha—since it would have been inconsistent with Nichiren's humility. Yoshiro Tamura holds that Nichiren considered himself not a bodhisattva but an emissary of the bodhisattvas, to spread the teaching of the Lotus Sutra. Among the passages Tamura quotes from the letters Nichiren wrote in the last six years of his life, one clearly states: "Nichiren's mind is not at all that of an emissary of the Buddha because I am a common man. But because I have been exiled twice by the three kinds of formidable enemies,[12] I look like an emissary of the Buddha. Although my mind is deeply afflicted with the three poisons,[13] and although I am a common man, I look like an emissary of the Buddha because I recite 'Nam-myoho Renge-kyo.' "[14]

NICHIREN SHOSHU'S VIEW OF NICHIREN

Of the doctrinal differences between Nichiren Shoshu and other Nichiren sects, the most important is that concerning the identity of Nichiren. While the other sects regard him as the *mappo*-era reincarnation of Jogyo Bosatsu, Nichiren Shoshu maintains that Nichiren was the *mappo no hombutsu* (the true Buddha of the *mappo* era).

In Chapter 16 of the Lotus Sutra, entitled "Nyorai Juryobon" (The Length of the Buddha's Life), the historical Buddha, addressing an infinitely large number of bodhisattvas in a mystical assembly, makes a startling revelation. He says

---

12 For the "three kinds of formidable enemies," see page 35.
13 The three poisons are avarice, irrationality, and stupidity.
14 Tamura, *op. cit.*, pp. 144–45.

(contrary both to the prevailing view and to what he himself had been saying) that although the Buddha attained the status of Enlightened One by meditating near the city of Buddha Gaya, he had actually become Buddha in the infinite past. In the style of exaggeration that characterizes the Lotus Sutra, the infinite length of time is stated to be 100 times 10,000 times 1,000,000 times one *nayuta* (100,000,000) times an infinite number of times one *kalpa* (8,000,000) years. The Buddha then elaborates on this fantastic length of time by using a no less fantastic figure. "Suppose," he says, "someone pulverized into dust 500 times 1,000 times 10,000 times 100,000 times one *nayuta* times one *asamkhya* [infinitely large number] of 10,000,000,000,000 universes [in Japanese, *sanzendaisen sekai*]. Then he goes eastward past 500 times 1,000 times 10,000 times 100,000 times 100,000,000 times one *asamkhya* of lands before dropping one particle of the dust, and thus he continues to eliminate all the dust particles." Then the Buddha asks his audience if it could conceive of, and calculate, the number of such universes to be covered before all the particles of the dust are spent. "Then pulverize all these universes—both those over which a particle was placed and those over which no dust particle was placed," the Buddha continues. "Then regard one particle as representing one *kalpa*. This is the length of time since I attained Buddhahood."

In short, the Buddha revealed that he had become a Buddha in the infinite past. Because of the reference to the numerals beginning with 500, this infinite length of time is known in Japanese as *gohyakujintengo*—literally, "five-hundred-dust-particle *kalpa*"—an abbreviated way of referring to an incalculable length of time.

The Buddha who attained Buddhahood in that remote past is known among Japanese Buddhists as Kuonjitsujo no Shaka Bosatsu, which may be simply translated into English as "the eternal Buddha."

This eternalization of the Buddha reflects the great affection and respect his disciples held for the historical Buddha, who was their teacher. He bequeathed his teachings to his followers for them to live by. But disciples who had believed in the Buddha's teachings through the person of Sakyamuni found it difficult to be content with abstract tenets. They created substitutes for the deceased—the conceptual, eternalized Buddha. Moreover, they created not only one such Buddha but many. By the time the Lotus Sutra assumed a written form,

A SCHEMATIC COMPARISON OF THE THEORIES
OF THE ETERNAL BUDDHA ACCORDING TO THE
NICHIREN SHOSHU AND OTHER NICHIREN SECTS

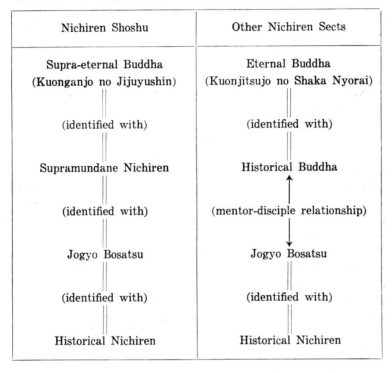

Nichiren Shoshu	Other Nichiren Sects
Supra-eternal Buddha (**Kuonganjo no Jijuyushin**)	Eternal Buddha (**Kuonjitsujo no Shaka Nyorai**)
(identified with)	(identified with)
Supramundane Nichiren	Historical Buddha
(identified with)	(mentor-disciple relationship)
Jogyo Bosatsu	Jogyo Bosatsu
(identified with)	(identified with)
Historical Nichiren	Historical Nichiren

however, the original Buddha, who had been eternalized, had superseded all other Buddhas as the ultimate and supreme one to which all other deities were subordinate.

The Nichiren sects accept the Lotus Sutra version of the eternal Buddha at face value. Nichiren himself seems to have accepted the description of the Buddha given in the sixteenth chapter of the Lotus Sutra.

Nichiren Shoshu's interpretation of the Lotus Sutra,

however, is unique in that it regards Nichiren as the reincarnation of an eternal Buddha who is distinct from the eternal Buddha worshiped by other Nichiren sects. This Buddha is known as both Kuonganjo no Jijuyushin and Gohyakujintengo no Jijuyushin Nyorai, terms used only in Nichiren Shoshu theology. The differentiation of Nichiren Shoshu's own "eternal Buddha" is achieved by the following semantic argument.

Nichiren, in his *Sokammonsho* of 1279, wrote that the Buddha had attained Buddhahood "prior to *gohyakujintengo*" —that is, in *kuonganjo* (the beginning of the eternal past), which predates *gohyakujintengo*. Nichiren Shoshu says that, compared with *kuonganjo*, even *gohyakujintengo* is "as recent as yesterday."

Thus, according to Nichiren Shoshu theology, the Buddha of *kuonganjo* is superior to the Buddha of *gohyakujintengo* (known as Kuonjitsujo no Shaka Nyorai in other Nichiren sects) because of his more remote origin. And Nichiren Shoshu identifies this Buddha of the past, "more remote than the eternal past," with Nichiren. This dogma was systematized by Nikkan (also known as Nichikan), one of the principal architects of the doctrine of Nichiren Shoshu, who was the twenty-sixth-generation high priest at Taiseki-ji. This doctrine of the eternal Buddha illustrates the mystical nature of Nichiren Shoshu theology, which can only be regarded as faith. *Kuonganjo* is held to be a time further in the past than *gohyakujintengo*. Yet, Nichiren Shoshu claims, the two concepts are not comparable. For were *kuonganjo* to refer to a finite moment in time, then the Buddha who emerged at that moment would be finite too. Hence "*kuonganjo* transcends time and therefore cannot be compared with *kuonjitsujo*."[15] In the language of Nichiren Shoshu theology, "to consider the life of the Buddha in terms of finite time is wrong; the life of every individual being is a manifestation of the life of the universe. Therefore *kuonganjo* and *now* are the same."[16]

For Nichiren Shoshu believers, such doctrines elaborate the basic distinction between their faith and that of other Nichiren

---

[15] Soka Gakkai Kyogakubu (Study Department, Soka Gakkai): *Bukkyo Tetsugaku Daijiten* (Encyclopedia of Buddhist Philosophy), Vol. 1, Tokyo, 1964, p. 969.
[16] *Ibid.*, Vol. 2 (1965), p. 495.

sects. The basic distinction is that Nichiren Shoshu regards Nichiren as the True Buddha in this age of *mappo;* other Nichiren sects, on the other hand, regard the True Buddha of this age to be the eternalized historical Buddha. To them, Nichiren was the reincarnation of Jogyo Bosatsu, a proxy of that Buddha.

This conviction of Nichiren Shoshu's theological superiority over other Nichiren sects undoubtedly contributes to the single-mindedness of Soka Gakkai members in the evangelical work they consider their goal—the spreading of their version of Nichiren's teachings.

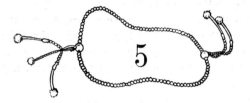

5

The Prewar History
of Soka Gakkai

Definition

Soka Gakkai may be defined simply as an association of lay adherents of Nichiren Shoshu. Like all other Buddhist sects in Japan, Nichiren Shoshu has its own hierarchy of priests, with temples throughout the country, its head temple being Taiseki-ji at Fujinomiya, Shizuoka Prefecture. Heading the clerical hierarchy is Nittatsu, high priest of the temple, to whom members of Nichiren Shoshu clergy and Soka Gakkai refer reverently as Nittatsu Shonin.[1]

Soka Gakkai, as a lay organization, has a lay hierarchy which does not overlap or conflict with that of the Nichiren Shoshu temples.[2] In this sense, Soka Gakkai is a *ko*, an association of lay worshipers of a deity, which happens to have a nationwide membership. Historically, the *ko* was a study session in which Buddhist priests read Buddhist scriptures in the imperial court during the Heian period (794–1192). Later the term was applied to any small, local group of adherents to a common faith. During the Muromachi period (1392–1573), *ko* were also formed by votaries of Shinto deities. The most popular were the Ise-ko, formed of worshipers of the Grand Shrine of Ise and found in local communities throughout

[1] *Shonin*, an honorific for a Buddhist priest in certain sects, roughly corresponds to "saint" in Christian terminology.
[2] On September 25, 1966, Soka Gakkai redesignated itself Nichiren Shoshu as far as its overseas chapters were concerned. This may have the unintended effect of blurring the clergy-laity distinction.

Japan. Members of a *ko* in those years took group excursions from their villages to Ise.[3]

The Nichiren sects too had many *ko* in medieval times. Named the Hokke-ko after the Lotus Sutra (Hoke-kyo),[4] these consisted of devout adherents of Nichiren and his canon. The martyrdom at Atsuhara, described in Chapter 3, involved a newly formed Hokke-ko of converts.

Although the Nichirenite order now known as Nichiren Shoshu was a minor sect in its first seven centuries of existence, it had its own *ko* in its few score temple parishes. When a new nationwide *ko* of Nichiren Shoshu believers—Soka Gakkai— emerged after World War II, delicate problems arose concerning its relationship with the existing *ko,* whose total membership was about 300,000. In the eyes of members of the old *ko,* Soka Gakkai was an upstart. Some Nichiren Shoshu temples, in fact, were often reluctant to administer the rites of admission to the faith to members of Soka Gakkai. Such an attitude was understandable, for converts to Nichiren Shoshu who were Soka Gakkai members did not identify themselves with the existing *ko* of their respective temples.

With the expansion of the new organization, however, the problems vanished. Nichijun, the sixty-fifth-generation high priest of Taiseki-ji, did his best to harmonize the relationship between the old *ko* and Soka Gakkai and to unify them as one national organization of lay adherents to the sect. Thus on April 19, 1958, Nichijun posthumously appointed Josei Toda, the second president of Soka Gakkai, *sokoto* (general head of *ko*). The *sokoto* technically heads all the Nichiren Shoshu *ko* in Japan, among which Soka Gakkai happens to be the largest single group. Likewise, on April 1, 1964, Nittatsu, Nichijun's successor, appointed Daisaku Ikeda, present president of Soka Gakkai, to the same post.

---

[3] In its further development, the *ko* as a form of social organization acquired an entirely new, nonreligious role. Many *ko* were formed as mutual-credit societies in which the members pooled their resources for mutual financial assistance. Many of these *ko,* religious or social, disappeared during World War II, when conditions made it difficult for them to function normally.

[4] The Lotus Sutra is known in Japan as Hoke-kyo, but a *ko* of its worshipers is a Hokke-ko, even though *hoke* and *hokke* are represented by identical ideographs.

Not a "New Religion"

Many Japanese consider Soka Gakkai to be one of the *shinko shukyo* (new religions) of Japan. This term is generally used to refer to those religions which have grown rapidly among the masses of modern Japan since about 1905 and whose doctrines are independent of, or at best only remotely related to, any of the three established religions of Japan, namely Shinto, Buddhism, and Christianity. Furthermore, the founder of a "new religion" usually claims to be a savior, healer, or prophet, and to be the sole source of religious authority for his or her organization. In short, in these "new religions" the founders are regarded as superhuman beings or "living gods."

Of the many "new religions" that emerged before World War II, only a few have survived to the present. Some, crushed in the 1930's and early 1940's by the government, were revived after the war. But the postwar moral hiatus in defeated Japan gave birth to many more "new religions," some of which are already dead or dying. Soka Gakkai, however, bears no resemblance to these "new religions" in their chief characteristics, for its doctrine is not new, being the teachings of Nichiren, and its founder Makiguchi did not claim divinity, sanctity, or any supernatural endowments. He merely interpreted the teachings of Nichiren and attempted, with considerable success, to persuade others of their truth.

Relations with Nichiren Shoshu

Among the various Nichiren sects and subsects founded over the seven centuries since Nichiren's time, Nichiren Shoshu was, until recently, one of the most insignificant, with a relatively small following. A survey conducted by the Religions Bureau of the Ministry of Education at the end of 1939 showed that there were only seventy-five temples of Nichiren Shoshu throughout Japan, while the temples of all other Nichiren sects and subsects totaled 4,962. Similarly, the total number of priests in the Nichiren Shoshu temples was fifty-two, while those of other Nichiren sects numbered 4,451 in all. (See table on following page.)

COMPARISON OF NICHIREN SHOSHU AND OTHER NICHIREN SECTS IN 1939[5]

	Number of temples	Number of priests	Number of danto (parishioners)[6]	Number of shinto (adherents)[7]
Nichiren Shoshu	75	52	45,332	40,209
Other Nichiren sects and subsects	4,962	4,451	2,074,530	1,318,521

As of January 1969, however, the Nichiren Shoshu temples numbered 319, including four located outside Japan. Temples built by Soka Gakkai and dedicated to Nichiren Shoshu—at the rate of from ten to twenty a year—account for most of the increase. Today Taiseki-ji, the head temple of Nichiren Shoshu, is undoubtedly the most prosperous of all the Buddhist temples of Japan, with approximately fifteen thousand votaries visiting it daily during eleven months of the year. (This statement leaves aside the temples that attract legions of tourists each year, such as those of Kyoto.)

FOUNDER MAKIGUCHI

This transformation of a relatively obscure Japanese Buddhist sect would not have occurred but for the schoolteacher Tsunesaburo Makiguchi and his fortuitous conversion to Nichiren Shoshu.

Makiguchi was born on June 6, 1871,[8] in Arahama-mura,

[5] Daisaku Ikeda: *Ningen Kakumei* (The Human Revolution), Seikyo Shimbun-sha, Tokyo, 1965, Vol. 1, pp. 239–40. Ikeda quotes the *Mainichi Nenkan* (Mainichi Almanac), 1942. Kazuo Kasahara, in his *Kakumei no Shukyo: Ikko Ikki to Soka Gakkai* (The Religions of Revolution: The Ikko Uprising and Soka Gakkai), Jimbutsu Orai-sha, Tokyo, 1964, gives the number of Nichiren Shoshu priests as of 1942 as 212, that of temples as 75, and the total number of *danto* and *shinto* as 87,041.

[6] *Danto* means a person who believes in the doctrine of a particular religious sect, entrusts funeral and related services to the temple to which he belongs as a parishioner, and protects the temple with his influence or financial resources.

[7] *Shinto* (not to be confused with Shinto, a religion) means the same as *danto*, with the exception that the *shinto* does not entrust his temple with funeral and related services.

[8] The date is by the lunar calendar which was in force in Japan until November 8, 1872.

Niigata Prefecture, a hamlet on the shore of the Sea of Japan. Arahama means "desolate beach," and Makiguchi's home village was indeed a bleak and poverty-stricken community. Fishing was difficult for the villagers because the offshore waters were rough, and rice paddies on land were scarce. Makiguchi was the first son of Chomatsu Watanabe and, by Japanese custom, should have received his family name. But at the age of three he was adopted into the family of Zendayu Makiguchi, his uncle-in-law.

A bright child, Makiguchi topped his class through the compulsory four years of primary school. Then he went to Otaru, Hokkaido, where his uncle Shiroji Watanabe lived. Because his foster parents could not afford to send him to high school, Makiguchi worked as an errand boy at the local police station. There he studied on his own in order to pass the government examination which would qualify him to take an entrance examination for college. The chief of police, impressed with the lad's industry and ambition, took him to Sapporo, the capital of Hokkaido, when he was transferred. There Makiguchi was enrolled in Sapporo Normal School as a third-year student and passed the government examination which qualified him in secondary-school geography and pedagogy. Upon graduation he taught in the primary school attached to his alma mater.

As his interest in geography deepened, Makiguchi resolved to become a geographer, and he wrote a dissertation on geography which he brought with him to Tokyo in 1901. He was then thirty years old. He called upon Shigetaka Shiga (1863–1927), a geographer, who is said to have been impressed with his young visitor's creative view and helped him to publish his manuscript.

Makiguchi's work on geography was remarkable in that he was interested primarily in the relationship between nature and man. Japanese geographers of the time were chiefly concerned with describing the physical features of the earth. Makiguchi had originally intended to entitle his book *Shakai Chirigaku* (Social Geography). But in the political climate of Japan at the turn of the century, the word *shakai* (society) was "dangerous" because it was taken to imply—usually without justification—*shakaishugi* (socialism), then an anathema to the government. Consequently, Makiguchi called his first opus, a 995-page tome published in 1903, *Jinsei Chirigaku* (Human Life Geography). The views elaborated in *Jinsei Chirigaku* on the relationship between man and his environment proved to be the source of Makiguchi's theory of value.

The book sold well and, according to his biographer, "transformed overnight the geographical world of Japan."[9] It had eight printings before 1911. Having thus produced a creditable academic work without formal education in the field, Makiguchi wanted to make his career as a geographer. But the academic circles of Japan proved decidedly unfriendly to the young self-made scholar. Makiguchi had to earn his living by working for the publisher of an educational magazine for girls. Later he edited school textbooks on geography for the Ministry of Education, then managed a correspondence school for girls which, after two years, was so seriously in debt that Makiguchi had to find other employment. To support his family, which by 1909 had increased to five children, Makiguchi returned to teaching. He taught over the next twenty years, first as deputy principal, later as principal.

In 1920, while Makiguchi was principal of Nishimachi Primary School in today's Taito Ward, Tokyo, a young man named Jin'ichi Toda from Hokkaido joined the teaching staff. Thereafter Toda was to follow in Makiguchi's footsteps.

Makiguchi kept up his study of geography while extending his interests to anthropology and folklore. During vacations in 1909 and 1910, for instance, he conducted studies of rural community life in Yamanashi Prefecture and Kyushu with the folklore expert Kunio Yanagida. However, his duties as school principal left Makiguchi so little time for extracurricular activities that he suffered frustration and unhappiness, often apparent to his colleagues.[10]

During his twenty years as a schoolteacher and principal, however, Makiguchi also devoted himself to his studies in educational theory, which he termed *soka kyoikugaku* (value-creating educational theory).

Makiguchi was obviously dissatisfied with the educational

9 Yoshihei Kodaira: *Soka Gakkai*, Otori Shoin, Tokyo, 1962, p. 65.
10 Shigeyoshi Murakami: *Soka Gakkai, Komeito*, Aoki Shoten, Tokyo, 1967, pp. 94–95.

theories then prevalent in Japan, which were based on European philosophical idealism. His approach was pragmatic and rationalist, derived from his own educational experience. But it was bound to clash with the "orthodox" theory of government educational authorities, who wanted to establish a highly centralized educational system. While Makiguchi was teaching primary school, the government was building up its bureaucratic control of school education.

Although he was recognized as an able teacher, Makiguchi's uncompromising attitude toward the authorities created problems. His clashes with officials of the Ministry of Education, school inspectors, ward assemblymen, city councilmen, and top officials of the city of Tokyo were frequent and resulted in his frequent transfers from one school to another.

In 1928, he was transferred to the post of principal of Niibori Primary School in Azabu, in today's Minato Ward, Tokyo, scheduled for closure in one year. The appointment, therefore, meant his dismissal with a year's notice. After this transfer, Makiguchi prepared to publish the educational theory he had developed during his teaching career. He retired from teaching in 1929.

At the home he had built in Mejiro, Tokyo, Makiguchi devoted himself to the publication of his twelve-volume educational treatise, which he entitled *Soka Kyoikugaku Taikei* (The Value-Creating Pedagogical System). The first volume was published in 1930, followed by the second in 1931, the third in 1932, and the fourth in 1934. The projected subsequent volumes, however, were not completed.

The colophon at the end of the first volume identified the publisher as Soka Kyoiku Gakkai (Value-Creating Educational Society)—the first mention of the term *soka kyoikugaku* in print. (The compound *gaku + kai* is pronounced "gakkai.") Thus Soka Gakkai today considers November 18, 1930—the publication date of this first volume—the founding date of its prewar predecessor, although formal inauguration came later.

Among the celebrities who gave their blessing to Makiguchi's publication venture was Tsuyoshi Inukai,[11] who wrote a

---

[11] Inukai (1855–1932) was prime minister of Japan from December 13, 1931, to May 15, 1932, when he was assassinated by a group of ultranationalists.

calligraphic epigraph in classic Chinese. It said: "There is no person in this world who cannot be taught; there is no person who ought not to be taught." The aphorism sums up Makiguchi's belief that everyone should have educational opportunity and his claim that he could make a superior student out of a poor one.

Another celebrity wrote a foreword for Makiguchi. This was Dr. Inazo Nitobe, of *Bushido* fame. Nitobe's words of praise, dated October 1930, read in part:

> I have often been involved with education and am at present still engaged in the task. I have always felt extremely dissatisfied with Japanese education and regretted the fact that it lacks creativity.
>
> In order to reform our educational system, it would be necessary first of all to rebuild our view of its purpose. Educational methods must then be reformed on the basis of the newly found purpose. . . . Few of those who regret the present educational system of our country object to the proposal for creative education. . . . Yet, the concept of "creativity" could be of infinite variety. Educationists and theoreticians have expounded their theories in their books and in their lectures, but none has so far convinced me of the excellence of his theory. . . .
>
> Now Mr. Makiguchi, who with his earlier *Human Life Geography* won acclaim overnight for his outstanding scholarship, presents a value-creating educational theory, based on his many years of experience and thinking, to the present-day educational world that is in a state of helpless confusion. Having read a synopsis of Mr. Makiguchi's value-creating educational theory, I have been astounded by the superiority of his thought and the comprehensiveness of his knowledge based on facts. Having learned that the author of *Human Life Geography* is still hale and hearty, I wish to congratulate him on his good health. I am firmly of the opinion that Mr. Makiguchi's value-creating educational theory is a Japanese educational theory, to which I had long looked forward. Furthermore, it is a masterwork whose advent our contemporaries have long awaited.[12]

Makiguchi's educational theory, however, was hardly put to the test. The only teacher to put it on trial was Jin'ichi Toda,

[12] Tsunesaburo Makiguchi: *Kachiron* (Theory of Value), supplemented by Josei Toda, Soka Gakkai, Tokyo, 1953, pp. 248–50.

who applied the theory to the pupils of his private school, Jishu Gakkan, which he used as an educational laboratory to "produce great educational results."[13]

Today, however, Soka Gakkai has an opportunity to put the late founder's educational theory into practice on a grand scale. As one of its numerous nonreligious activities, Soka Gakkai has an extensive educational program. In April 1968, it opened its own Soka secondary schools and plans to establish Soka University in 1971.

Had it not been for an apparently minor incident in the life of Makiguchi, however, today's Soka Gakkai would not exist. When he was principal of Shirogane Primary School in mid-1928, he was visited by a reporter for a trade paper who was a Nichiren Shoshu adherent. The reporter introduced Makiguchi to a fellow believer named Sokei Mitani, principal of a business high school in Tokyo's Mejiro Ward.

An influential member of the Nichiren Shoshu ko of Jozai-ji temple in Ikebukuro, Tokyo, Mitani converted Makiguchi to his sect. Although Makiguchi's family background in Niigata was that of Nichiren Shu,[14] his attachment to his family religion was apparently too tenuous to prove an obstacle to his joining Nichiren Shoshu. He had also shown a mild interest in Christianity, influenced by a Christian classmate in his Sapporo Normal School days and later by Dr. Nitobe. Evidently, however, it was not serious enough to convert him. Whatever religious thirst Makiguchi felt was sated by his encounter with Nichiren Shoshu.

A New World View

Makiguchi's theory of education, put forward in the four

---

[13] Tokyo Daigaku Hoke-kyo Kenkyukai (Tokyo University Lotus Sutra Study Society): *Nichiren Shoshu Soka Gakkai*, Sankibo Busshorin, Tokyo, 1967 (revised edition), p. 271.

[14] Murakami, *op. cit.*, p. 96. A Soka Gakkai publication, however, claims that after joining Nichiren Shoshu, Makiguchi found in his Niigata home an old picture of "Nichiren of Nichiren Shoshu." This publication, quoted in Tokyo Daigaku Hoke-kyo Kenkyukai, *op. cit.*, p. 270, goes on to say: "It is said that President Makiguchi, who realized this after joining Nichiren Shoshu, was profoundly moved by this coincidence. . . . There was something inevitable in the fact that President Makiguchi founded Soka Kyoiku Gakkai."

volumes of his life work, is based on his own theory of value, which he expounded in the second volume of his work, entitled *Soka Kyoikugaku Taikei*. Because of its importance, Soka Gakkai reissued this volume, giving it the title *Kachiron* (Theory of Value), in September 1953, with a supplement by Josei Toda, the second president of Soka Gakkai and Makiguchi's successor.

Makiguchi's doctrine consists essentially of the three values he put forward to replace the conventional triad of truth, goodness, and beauty. His three values were *bi* (beauty), *ri* (gain), and *zen* (goodness).

A key element of his system of values is the premise that truth, traditionally the primary value, is not a value. To Makiguchi, truth and value are concepts on entirely different planes. He defines truth as "a concept which objectifies the relationship between a being such as man and something in his environment." Value, on the other hand, is a subjective relationship between the two—that is, man and the thing. As a simple illustration, he says that the statement "Here is a horse" is a truth if it conforms to a particular reality. But if a person says about the horse, "This horse is beautiful" or "precious," then it is a statement of value.

A truth could not be created; it could only be discovered. Value, however, could be created or discovered. Makiguchi was primarily concerned with the values he believed must be created.

Truth or falsehood have no relationship to human life, according to Makiguchi. But values do, because they represent man's relationship with his environment. He was attempting to distinguish value judgments from factual judgments, or subjective responses from objective responses.

Makiguchi's three values require elaboration. What he calls *bi* (beauty) is sensual pleasure, derived through man's senses. *Ri* (gain) derives from the relationship between a person and an object that contributes to the preservation and development of his life. *Zen* (goodness) is the personal conduct which intentionally contributes to the development of the society of which he is a member. In other words, his "goodness" is public good or utility.[15] The antitheses of *bi*, *ri*, and *zen* are

[15] Makiguchi, *op. cit.*, p. 16.

shu (unpleasantness or ugliness), *gai* (harm), and *aku* (evil).[16] Whether something is good or evil depends on the particular society, and what is gain or harm depends on the individual. Therefore, argues Makiguchi, an action by an individual which brings him gain could well be an evil to the society of which he is a member.

Makiguchi also took pains to distinguish cognition from evaluation, offering the following example of confusion between value and factual judgments:

> A pupil asks his teacher, "What is this?" And if the teacher says: "You mean to say you still don't know what it is?" he is definitely confusing the processes of cognition and evaluation. The pupil who asked the teacher the question did not seek a judgment on his own competence. He was seeking information, not an evaluation of his own ability. The teacher who does not answer the pupil's real question but diverts his attention to something else is intimidating the child, and yet he thinks he is thus helping the child's comprehension. . . . Under a teacher of this kind, a poor pupil cannot but become even a poorer pupil.[17]

Makiguchi says that while truth never changes, value does. Something that is essential to A is of no use at all to B, or at least of far less use to him than to A. Even the value of one thing to one person may vary from time to time. "This is illustrated by the fact that morality differs between the present and past [in one society] and between two societies."

Clearly, Makiguchi was a relativist in the theory of value, and, in fact, he rejected the absolute "religious value" advocated by the contemporary German philosopher Wilhelm Windelband (1848–1915), who upheld, besides truth, beauty, and goodness, a fourth absolute—namely God.[18]

This raises the question of how Makiguchi, who categorically rejects the concept of absolute "religious value," reconciled his relativism with his faith in a religion that claims to be absolute truth.

An answer to this question is given in Makiguchi's *Kachiron* as "supplemented" by his pupil Toda. In one section, the

---

[16] These three sets of values and their antitheses, in fact, form the common Japanese compounds *bishu* (beauty and ugliness), *rigai* (interest—or benefit—and harm), and *zen'aku* (good and evil).

[17] Makiguchi, *op. cit.*, p. 20. [18] *Ibid.*, p. 166.

author's tone of argument suddenly changes, and his abstract, nonreligious, philosophic discourse is abruptly followed by references to Nichiren and the Lotus Sutra. It appears that this section of Makiguchi's original, published in 1931, was "supplemented" by Toda in the 1953 reprint edition, since in this section there are references to nuclear physics and the atom bomb that Makiguchi obviously would not have mentioned.

The author argues that all religions other than Nichiren Shoshu contradict scientific knowledge and logic because they are not "true religions."

> For instance, it is not strange that it is impossible to give a scientific explanation of Christianity—according to which a virgin gave birth to a child and [Christ] was found walking around after his death—because its basis is erroneous. Therefore if one must claim such a religion to be correct, he must despise science, and hence the religion and science must find themselves in conflict with each other.[19]

There is only one religion in the world that "does not contradict science and, furthermore, is scientific and logical and could be proved so empirically. It is supreme and unadulterated."

"The object of this philosophy of religion," says Makiguchi, "is human life. It deals with the life of man, the life of everything, the life of society and of a country and even the life of this great universe." Such a religion is "similar to science" because science contributes to the happiness of human life, and the "supreme theorem of this religion," too, may be put into practice to gain the happy life of man.[20]

A few lines later, reference is suddenly made to the Lotus Sutra as the "supreme study" by the Buddha. The seeming incongruity between Makiguchi the relativist and Makiguchi (and/or Toda) the absolutist may be resolved by the following reasoning. Makiguchi is a relativist concerning the practice of the three values he recognizes. But he is an absolutist in that he holds one specific religion, Nichiren Shoshu, to be the only logical and valid faith which could enable man to create these three categories of value.

[19] *Ibid.*, p. 168.   [20] *Ibid.*, pp. 169–70.

Makiguchi relates his axiology with religion in still another way. He reiterates that "the purpose of life is the pursuit of happiness, and happiness consists of values."[21] And "values and happiness cannot be considered without religion."[22] But "religion," according to Makiguchi, is not an object of cognition but of evaluation—that is, something to be believed in and practiced.

Yet Makiguchi rejects all religions other than his own Buddhism on the basis of his own theory of values. Since the "substance of one's happiness consists of *bi, ri*, and *zen*," one might be satisfied with oneself if one acquired *bi* and *ri*. But "there can be no true happiness for an individual until *zen*—that is, good or benefit to society—is attained." The religion Makiguchi advocates may not give the individual spiritual satisfaction or peace of mind, but it must provide society as a whole with what it holds to be desirable.[23]

To justify his claim for the "supremacy" of Nichiren Shoshu, Makiguchi cites the Buddhist doctrine of *ichinen sanzen*, describing it as "a profound philosophy that far transcends every scientific study and makes the true character of human life clear."[24]

BEGINNINGS OF SOKA KYOIKU GAKKAI

Despite the first reference in print to Soka Kyoiku Gakkai in 1930, the organization Soka Kyoiku Gakkai was not formally founded until early 1937. About sixty people attended the inaugural meeting held at the restaurant Kikusuitei in Tokyo's

---

21 *Ibid.*, p. 173.   22 *Ibid.*, pp. 178–79.

23 *Ibid.*, p. 213.   This statement sheds light on the political interest of Soka Gakkai—expressed in its own political party, Komeito. According to Soka Gakkai, a "true" religion must not bring happiness to individuals alone but to community and society as well. If a religion is primarily concerned with the personal happiness of the believer—Zen Buddhism, for instance—it need not intervene in the organization and activities of society or state. But if its concern is the well-being of all members of society, then it needs, in today's world, a political implement to achieve what it believes will benefit the community. Daisaku Ikeda, president of Soka Gakkai, disagrees with this interpretation, however, and gives a different reason for Soka Gakkai's participation in the nation's politics through Komeito. (See page 176.)

24 *Ibid.*, p. 230. For an explanation of the doctrine of *ichinen sanzen*, see Chapter 4.

Azabu. This was the first "general meeting." The second was held three years later, in 1940, at the Gunjin Kaikan in Kudan, Tokyo. By then, membership had increased to "three to four hundred." Thereafter, the organization held semiannual meetings at which members reported the results of their educational research programs and their personal experiences. That membership should have increased six or seven times between 1937 and 1940 is regarded by Soka Gakkai as remarkable, since these were the years of "national emergency," when the militaristic government was imposing Shinto and emperor worship on the people as part of its nationalist drive. The growth of Soka Kyoiku Gakkai reached its peak in 1941, when members' study sessions were held regularly and branches were established in cities other than Tokyo.

On July 20, 1941, the organization began to publish its organ *Kachi Sozo* (Creation of Values). As of that time, it claimed three thousand members, ranging from Hokkaido in the north to Kyushu in the south.

Since 1936, Makiguchi had held an annual summer seminar. In 1941, the seminar lasted a week, from August 7 through 13, and was attended by 180 persons. On August 20, the second issue of *Kachi Sozo* was published and, on October 20, the third. On November 2, about four hundred members attended the autumn general meeting at the Kyoiku Kaikan in Hitotsubashi, Tokyo. In December, a combined issue of Nos. 4 and 5 of *Kachi Sozo* appeared. In the same month, Japan declared war on the United States and Great Britain.

With the coming of war, the government's attempts to unify the "thoughts" of the people and to merge the various Buddhist sects in the cause of national unity became ever more intense. Shinto worship was declared essential for every citizen regardless of his personal religious feelings. The sanctity of the sun goddess at Ise as the supreme object of such worship was stressed.

In 1940, the government had enacted the Religious Organizations Law, which gave the state control over religions and enabled it to make use of all religions in the war effort. A specific objective of this policy was to unite all Nichiren sects and subsects. As the table on page 71 clearly shows, Nichiren

Shoshu was a minority among all the Nichiren sects. Inevitably, the leaders of the wartime government wanted this apparently insignificant, dissident group absorbed into the dominant Nichiren Shu. Some of the Nichiren Shoshu priests favored a merger, and indeed one of them, Jimon Ogasawara, is said to have "compromised with the militarists by holding that Shinto was more important than Buddhism."[25]

Both clerical and lay Nichiren Shoshu believers, however, at their joint meeting, decided against a merger and managed to acquire government authorization to remain independent. This was in April 1943. Makiguchi urged Nichiren Shoshu believers to take for granted the authorization and declared that they should "exhort the government, ban the evil religions, and spread the correct faith."[26]

In the meantime, other religious groups succumbed to the pressure of the government. They all worshiped the tablets of the Grand Shrine of Ise to prove their loyalty to the emperor system and the state. For the ardent members of Soka Kyoiku Gakkai, however, there was no object of worship other than Nichiren, the supreme and absolute deity. But the philosophy of Makiguchi and his followers lacked neither patriotism nor nationalism. They maintained that Japan would prosper once the state recognized Nichiren Shoshu, the "only correct religion." In fact, this was the same attitude that Nichiren took seven centuries before. He urged the rulers of the land to espouse what he believed was the only correct religion, and then, he thought, the nation would enjoy peace and prosperity.

Kachi Sozo was banned after the publication of the ninth issue, dated May 10, 1942. Even then, Makiguchi and other leaders of Soka Kyoiku Gakkai continued their *shakubuku* (proselytizing) activities. But as Allied air raids intensified, evening discussion meetings, a key means of winning converts, were canceled by frequent alerts, which forced city dwellers to turn out the lights and enter air-raid shelters. Yet six to seven hundred members attended the spring general meeting of 1943, held in Tokyo, and the society claimed a national membership of three thousand at that time.

---

[25] Kodaira, *op. cit.*, p. 68.   [26] *Ibid.*, p. 68.

Undaunted by government suppression and hostile surveil-
lance, Makiguchi continued to preach that Japan's only
salvation from the formidable adversary (the Allied Powers)
lay in faith in Nichiren. He even dared to say: "How is it
possible to save the country by praying to the sun goddess?"
No doubt Makiguchi had in mind Nichiren's fearless behavior
during the national crisis seven hundred years before.

By that time, some of the priests at Taiseki-ji, the head
temple of Nichiren Shoshu, were ready to compromise with
the State Shintoists in the government. After two Soka Kyoiku
Gakkai members were arrested on June 5, 1943, for "excesses
in the language they used in trying to *shakubuku* their
neighbors,"[27] the priests of Taiseki-ji ordered Makiguchi and
other lay leaders to visit the temple and asked them: "Why
not tell all your members to accept the sacred tablet of the
Grand Shrine of Ise?" (In those years, a sacred tablet of Ise
was to be worshiped by every family in Japan.)

Makiguchi refused to compromise, demonstrating stronger
devotion to his faith than some of the priests exhibited. After
the meeting, Makiguchi is said to have lamented:

> This is not a question of whether one particular Buddhist sect
> perishes. I deplore the fact that the nation is about to perish.
> I fear the sorrows Nichiren Daishonin [Nichiren the Great
> Saint] would feel [if such a time should come]. This is the
> time [as Nichiren did in his own time] to teach the national
> leaders what the correct religion is. What are [the priests at
> Taiseki-ji] afraid of?

Makiguchi's refusal to worship the sun goddess ended in his
arrest on July 6, 1943. His chief pupil, Toda, was arrested on
the same day. All together, twenty-one leaders of Soka Kyoiku
Gakkai were taken into custody, which virtually broke up the
group. Of the twenty-one leaders, fourteen were in Tokyo, four
in Kanagawa Prefecture, and three in Fukuoka Prefecture.

Under either torture or intensive interrogation, many of
these leaders renounced their faith in Nichiren Shoshu before
their trial was finished. The official suppression and the losing war Japan was fighting prevented members—scattered
throughout the country—from maintaining contact with one
another. Hence the total suspension of the society's activities

[27] *Ibid.*, p. 69.

for two years until the end of World War II. Soka Kyoiku Gakkai, which claimed a national membership of five thousand in the summer of 1943, had been wiped out.

On November 18, 1944, at the age of seventy-three, Makiguchi died of malnutrition and old age at the Sugamo Detention House in Tokyo. In *Ningen Kakumei*, Daisaku Ikeda reveals that, while in jail, Makiguchi, despite his failing health, refused to renounce his faith in the face of "cruel interrogation, repeated torture, and humiliation which ignored the basic human rights." Prison officials urged Makiguchi to move to the infirmary within the detention house. Although critically ill, Makiguchi refused to leave his cell. On November 17, 1944, he at last agreed to go to the infirmary, but he walked unaided, refusing the assistance of a guard.

In the infirmary, Makiguchi was examined by a doctor but refused to take medicine, and the following morning he died peacefully. The official record at the Sugamo Detention House notes that Tsunesaburo Makiguchi was "released on November 18, 1944." Makiguchi was released as a corpse, which one of his pupils carried on his back to Makiguchi's home.[28]

The sentences against the arrested members of Soka Kyoiku Gakkai were not passed until the following year—just before the end of World War II. By that time, of the twenty-one originally arrested, sixteen had been acquitted because they had renounced their faith. One person was not indicted. But Toda was given a suspended sentence of three years' penal servitude and released on July 3, 1945. Two others who received suspended two-year sentences were also released.

---

[28] Ikeda, *op. cit.*, pp. 189–90. An American writer who interviewed Daisaku Ikeda (although Soka Gakkai says he did not) wrote as follows on the circumstances of Makiguchi's death: ". . . I received a very interesting piece of information [from Ikeda]. Makiguchi had *not* died in prison but had been released, because of his poor health and advanced age, and died shortly thereafter, Ikeda explained offhandedly, thus denying one of the most widely broadcast and accepted legends about his organization—or perhaps simply launching a new one." (J. M. Flagler: "A Reporter at Large: A Chanting in Japan," *The New Yorker*, November 26, 1966, p. 187.) The basis of this statement is probably the fact that Makiguchi was transferred from his isolation cell to the infirmary the day before his death—information which was mistranslated to the American interviewer.

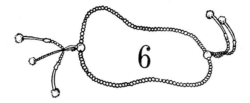

Toda, the Second President

TODA'S EARLY LIFE

The man chiefly responsible for the existence today of Soka Gakkai was born on February 11, 1900, the eleventh son of a poor fisherman in the village of Shioya, Ishikawa Prefecture, which, like Niigata, Makiguchi's birthplace, faces the Sea of Japan.

In 1904, when Toda, named Jin'ichi (which he later changed first to Jogai, then to Josei), was four years old, his family moved to Hokkaido. They settled in a small fishing village called Atsuta in Atsuta County in the province of Ishikari. When he graduated from primary school there, Toda found employment with a wholesaler in Sapporo. Working conditions were poor, but Toda managed to study in his spare time and, in three years, to pass the examination that qualified him, aged seventeen, as a substitute primary-school teacher.[1]

In June 1918, Toda was appointed a teacher at Mayachi Primary School, in a remote corner of the coal mining town of Yubari, Hokkaido. A year later, he passed the examination which fully qualified him as a primary-school teacher and was assigned to a sixth-grade class. Since he was at Mayachi only twenty-one months, he did not teach a large number of pupils. Even so, some of Toda's ex-pupils who are still living are reported to remember him clearly, describing him as "an excellent teacher, though at times he was very stern." They say too that Toda abruptly vanished from Mayachi one cold

[1] This description of Toda's early life is based largely on Daisaku Ikeda: *Ningen Kakumei* (The Human Revolution), Vol. 2, Seikyo Shimbun-sha, Tokyo, 1966.

morning in February 1920. Just before the first morning class, his pupils were as usual making a great deal of noise when the teacher's door opened. Toda's bespectacled face appeared. He looked over the classroom without a word, turned back, closed the door quietly, and was not seen again. Even when the pupils were to graduate in the following month, their teacher did not appear.

Records at Mayachi Primary School, recently checked by Soka Gakkai, yielded no clue to the sudden, unexplained departure of the young schoolteacher from the Hokkaido mining town. It is only recorded that he retired on March 31, 1920.

In early March, Toda was in Tokyo. For months, however, he could not find suitable employment. Meanwhile, in April, he wrote to his former pupils in Hokkaido, asking them to forgive him for missing their graduation ceremony. "You must have been astonished because I suddenly disappeared. But there were unavoidable reasons. Your teacher has not forgotten you." He is said to have corresponded with his former Hokkaido charges for about fifteen years.

Job-hunting in Tokyo, he came to know working students who were also from Hokkaido. One of them knew Makiguchi, then principal of Nishimachi Primary School in Tokyo's Shitaya district. In mid-August 1920, Toda called at Makiguchi's home with a letter of introduction from the youth from Hokkaido.

Makiguchi was friendly to the fellow teacher from Hokkaido, who immediately asked to be employed at Makiguchi's school. "I can make a superior student out of any inferior one, no matter how bad he may be," Toda insisted. "If you hire me, Mr. Makiguchi, I am sure you will be glad that you did."

Makiguchi hired Toda, and the young schoolteacher, always eager to get ahead and improve himself, set himself a new goal: to pass the examination to qualify him to take an entrance examination for college. In those years, one seeking admission to college without a middle-school education had to prove scholarship equal to that of a fourth-year student in the five-year middle school. Toda attended evening classes at Kaisei Middle School. Among his classmates was a student named Seiichi Hosoi, who later became Nittatsu Hosoi, the sixty-sixth high priest of Taiseki-ji. This prewar relationship between Hosoi and Toda undoubtedly helped later to forge the close links between the Taiseki-ji clergy and the Soka Gakkai laity.

Toda passed the qualifying examination in 1922, but in the same year he quit teaching to become a life-insurance salesman. Although devoted to Makiguchi, who was his lifelong mentor, in those years Toda preferred a more lucrative occupation than primary-school teaching. In 1923, Toda and his wife, whom he had married a few years before, opened a tutoring school for primary-school pupils, called Jishu Gakkan, at Meguro.

A pupil who finished six-year primary school had to pass a competitive examination to enter a middle school, so there was a demand for such tutoring. At his private school, Toda put into practice Makiguchi's "value-creating educational theory."

In late 1923, the Todas had a baby girl, but she died six months later, and Toda is said to have wept the whole night, holding the infant's body. This was the first of a chain of tragedies to befall him. In 1925, his wife died of tuberculosis. Toda himself suffered from the same disease and was frequently incapacitated.

His fortunes improved, however, when he began to publish books to help pupils preparing for middle-school entrance examinations. One book on arithmetic proved highly successful; it sold more than one million copies.[2] The author's name was Jogai Toda—the first use of Toda's new name, which he was later to change again.

For the first time in his life, Toda was affluent. About the same time, a new phase of his career began. Following his mentor Makiguchi, Toda too espoused Nichiren Shoshu in 1928. When Makiguchi left teaching in 1930 to devote himself to the publication of *Soka Kyoikugaku Taikei*, Toda served as his publisher and printer. The signboard bearing the name of Soka Gakkai was hung over Toda's tutoring school, which by then had moved to Kamiosaki, Osaki-cho, Tokyo. Toda's business success enabled him to foot the organization's bills single-handed, while he served as chairman of the board of directors of Soka Kyoiku Gakkai.

2 Tokyo Daigaku Hoke-kyo Kenkyukai, *op. cit.*, p. 289.

Until his arrest in 1943, Toda appears to have been more interested in business than in religion. He used the profits from his successful publishing venture to diversify his business activities. He started a moneylending business and engaged in stockbroking at Kabuto-cho, Tokyo. A great lover of sakè, Toda enjoyed drinking parties with his employees and fellow worshipers of Nichiren. And he could well afford much merry-making. At the time of his arrest for his religious activities in the summer of 1943, businessman Toda controlled seventeen companies, with two more about to come under his wing.

Until he joined Nichiren Shoshu in 1928, Toda had sought a philosophy in other religions, including Christianity, but none had solved his problems about the meaning of life. But he was not then prepared to devote himself wholeheartedly to a religious movement, as he was to do after World II. The life of a business enterpriser was more agreeable to him.

Affirmation of his faith in Nichiren occurred while Toda was in jail. He himself described his turning point:

> Long ago, I lost a daughter shortly after her birth. In jail I recalled how I had suffered and grieved at that time. Because I had grieved so much over the child's death, I wondered what I would do if my wife died (who did die and I grieved her death) and what I would do if my parents died (and they did die in fact and I wept bitterly).
>
> I shuddered at these thoughts. And then I wondered what I would do when I faced my own death. I felt dizzy because of the uncertainty. After that, I ceaselessly sought the way to salvation by becoming a Christian or by reading the Amida-kyo.[3] But I was never able to find an answer to the question of life which would really satisfy me.
>
> I went through this agony once again while in an isolation cell in jail. Having always been interested in the studies of science and mathematics, I could not believe in anything which was not logically convincing. So I devoted myself to reading the Hoke-kyo [Lotus Sutra] and the sacred writings of Nichiren Daishonin.[4]

[3] The Amida-kyo (Amida Sutra; in Sanskrit, Skhavati-vyuha) is the bible of the Shin and Jodo sects of Buddhism. Nichiren discredited it by holding that the Lotus Sutra was the only sutra containing the true teachings of the Buddha.

[4] Josei Toda: "Seimei no Honshitsuron" (Thesis on the Essence of Life), which forms the first chapter of *Shakubuku Kyoten* (Shakubuku Manual), second edition, edited and published by the Study Department of Soka Gakkai, Tokyo, 1967, p. 3.

Early in 1944, Toda began chanting the *daimoku*—that is, the sacred phrase "Nam-myoho Renge-kyo"—more than ten thousand times a day. After two million repetitions, an "extremely strange sensation" seized him, and "a world which I could never see before unfolded itself in front of me." His body shaking with ecstatic joy, Toda stood in his cell and shouted to "all Buddhas, all bodhisattvas, and all common men of the world" that he had now found, at the age of forty-five, "the true meaning of life."[5]

About the same time, Makiguchi died. Toda had last seen his teacher shortly after their arrest in the previous summer, and he was not immediately told of his death, although he was held in the same detention house.

Toda learned of Makiguchi's death on January 8, 1945, when the public prosecutor interrogating him curtly told him: "Makiguchi is dead." Upon returning to his cell, Toda wept all night. "I had never thought there could be such a great sorrow as this," he said, recalling that day at the memorial service for Makiguchi on November 18, 1945, the first anniversary of his death. At the same time, Toda reaffirmed publicly his vow to devote the rest of his life to spreading the teachings of Nichiren.

The Reconstruction of the Organization

On July 3, 1945, after two years' detention, Toda, suffering from malnutrition, was released from Toyotama Prison, to which he had been transferred from Sugamo Detention House only three days before.

If prison life weakened him physically, however, it certainly did not break his spirit. When he returned to his home in a Tokyo devastated by Allied air raids, Toda "was burning with a desire for vengeance—not against the militarist government of Japan but against an invisible enemy who had caused his own suffering of more than two years as well as his teacher's death in jail and agony to tens of millions of his fellow countrymen."

[5] *Ibid.*, p. 4.

Despite his vow to devote himself to spreading Nichiren Shoshu, Toda's immediate interest was the reconstruction of his business empire. Before his arrest, his fortune amounted to "more than ¥6,000,000."[6] After two years in detention, he found his businesses shattered and a debt of "two million and hundreds of thousands of yen" awaiting him.

Even before Japan surrendered to the Allied Powers on August 15, 1945, Toda had set about rebuilding his finances. With ¥5,000 capital, borrowed from an old friend, he rented an office in Kamiosaki, Tokyo, and employed an office staff, including several former employees. His first postwar enterprise was a correspondence school for middle-school students in mathematics and science, Toda's special subjects. The *Asahi Shimbun* of August 23, 1945 (then printed in two pages on a single sheet of paper because of the paper shortage) carried on page one a single advertisement by the Nihon Shogakkan offering tutoring by correspondence in mathematics and science for students in the first three years of middle school. The advertised courses were to last six months, with two lessons and one exam each month. The total cost was ¥250, to be paid in advance.

Within a few days, money orders began to pour in, the daily total mounting from ¥2,000 to ¥5,000 to ¥10,000 and even higher. Years later, Toda recalled that his inspiration to tutor by correspondence had come to him on August 20, 1945—forty-nine days after he was paroled on July 3. In Buddhism, the forty-ninth day is auspicious.[7] "I had a feeling that something was going to happen," Toda reminisced. "And when the inspiration did come, I did not wait even ten minutes." Before the end of 1945, Toda had laid the foundations for rebuilding his business—a definite indication, he declared, of the benefit derived from faith in Nichiren.

Soka Kyoiku Gakkai, which Toda had helped Makiguchi to found and lead, was all but a total loss. Of the twenty-one persons arrested in 1943, Toda alone remained unbroken in spirit. Only the president, who died in jail, refusing to renounce his faith, and Toda himself had withstood the pressures of the militarist and ultranationalist regime of Japan. As for the

[6] At the official prewar exchange rate, this was about $1,500,000.
[7] See page 19.

thousands of rank-and-file members, there was no way of regaining contact with them. Yet, as news of Toda's release spread, some began to visit his business office. Several of Soka Gakkai's top leaders today were among those prewar members of Soka Kyoiku Gakkai who returned to Toda's leadership after the war.

In rebuilding the society of Nichiren worshipers, Toda based his policy on the bitter experience of seeing the prewar group disintegrate and its individual members backslide. He reasoned that Soka Kyoiku Gakkai had been weak in the doctrinal discipline of its members, and for his postwar attempt, he wanted to inculcate members with the teachings found in the Lotus Sutra. He opened a seminar on the sutra on January 1, 1946, at Taiseki-ji, with three followers. After January 5, he lectured three times a week at his office in Nishi Kanda in downtown Tokyo, where his Nihon Shogakkan had moved in mid-October 1945. The first floor of this modest two-story wooden structure was the business office; the second floor became the headquarters of his renewed religious activities. To symbolize his new start, Toda changed his name from Jogai to Josei (which means literally "castle righteousness").[8]

On May 1, 1946, at the first postwar meeting of leaders of the revived organization, it was agreed that Toda should serve, as before, as chairman of the board of directors. The post of president was left vacant. Fifteen chapters—ten in Tokyo and five in other areas—were recognized. On July 1, the organ *Kachi Sozo*, a mimeographed pamphlet, resumed publication. On June 11, Toda formed the Young Men's Division with eleven members—all new recruits. With a steady proselytizing campaign, Soka Gakkai—as the organization was now renamed—increased its membership by about two hundred new members in 1946 alone.

In these months, the membership drive was conducted primarily in the form of discussion meetings over which Toda himself and other leaders of the society presided. Toda also attached great importance to lectures on the Lotus Sutra and writings by Nichiren. Members invited newcomers to these

[8] In April 1951, Toda changed his name again. Although in sound it was the same—Josei—the ideograph for the sound *sei* was changed to one meaning "sacred" or "holy."

lectures and discussion meetings, where there were strenuous efforts to convert them.

Among the young men who joined Soka Gakkai in 1947 was Daisaku Ikeda, who has since succeeded Toda as president. In July 1947, Soka Gakkai began publication of its monthly *Daibyakurenge*, which replaced *Kachi Sozo*. *Seikyo Shimbun*, with three issues a month, was inaugurated in April 1951 and is now a daily.

Soka Gakkai's peak rate of growth came after Toda was inaugurated president on May 3, 1951. As chairman of the association's board of directors, Toda had not been devoting all his energies to spreading the teachings of Nichiren. He spent most working days on his business activities, limiting his religious activities to evenings and weekends.

Toda's early success in business, which he claimed was a divine reward, did not last. Even the correspondence school incurred heavy debts because of soaring inflation. The prepaid fee of ¥250 per person for the six-month course did not cover the cost of paper, printing, and other expenses, which continued to climb. Hence the increasing number of subscribers, instead of spelling a business success, brought financial difficulties. Toda decided to switch to publishing books. Among his publications were *Lectures on Democracy* and a number of popular novels. These sold well, but when Toda prepared a second printing, he found that the inflationary rise in production costs made reprinting uneconomical. Had he reissued the books at higher prices to cover costs, there was no assurance that they would sell as well as the first printing.

Toda tried to redeem the failure of his first two enterprises by publishing a magazine. He reasoned that a monthly magazine would be a more reliable venture than single book titles, and as the costs of production rose, he could raise the price of the magazine from month to month. His first magazine was named *Boken Shonen* (Adventure Boy), and it was followed by a monthly for women, named *Ruby*. Both were successful: the circulation of the former was more than 100,000 and of the latter, tens of thousands.

The success of these magazines, however, was short-lived. Japan's abnormal postwar economy had permitted speculative, fly-by-night enterprises to enjoy ephemeral prosperity. But as conditions became more normal, the major prewar publishing houses, ruined at the end of the war, slowly regained their footing as the paper mills resumed their activities. Many magazines whose publication had been suspended during the immediate postwar years were revived by these old publishing houses. And they presented formidable competition to Toda's publication business. During the middle of 1949, Toda's Nihon Shogakkan was receiving an increasing number of remainders of its magazines from the bookstores. By the end of October that year, the business had a deficit of millions of yen, and Toda was compelled to fold it up. As a way out of the business difficulty, he then switched to moneylending by heading a credit cooperative named Toko Kensetsu Shinyo Kumiai.

The new business venture, however, was also destined to prove a failure. The credit cooperative suffered from no dearth of demand for loans, but it lacked funds because not enough members of the cooperative could deposit money. Toda's efforts to find a new source of capital proved fruitless because all the potential investors whom he knew were understandably reluctant to invest in his new business. On August 23, 1950, the Ministry of Finance ordered the credit cooperative to suspend its business, thus ending Toda's financial enterprise. On November 12, 1950, Toda resigned as chairman of the board of directors of Soka Gakkai, giving his business failure as the reason. Shuhei Yajima succeeded him.

With the collapse of his business ventures, many of Toda's followers, including Soka Gakkai leaders, deserted him and the organization. But at the same time, Ikeda was brought into closer contact with Toda. Ikeda had joined Soka Gakkai in August 1947, and in January 1949 he left the printing company where he had been employed and went to work for Toda's Nihon Shogakkan. Ikeda remained loyal to Toda, and, working as his secretary, he won Toda's absolute confidence and trust.

Although Toda escaped indictment in connection with his credit cooperative, he lost the entrepreneurial foothold he had built up after the war. He himself regarded his misfortune as divine retribution for his failure to devote himself to leading Soka Gakkai.

In late 1950, Toda decided to rectify his error by taking the post of president of the association, left vacant since Makiguchi's death. In January 1951, he informed his fellow believers of his intention, and he was formally inaugurated on May 3 of the same year.

"I really disliked the idea of becoming president of Soka Gakkai," Toda reminisced in 1952. "Perhaps it is more truthful to say that I was afraid of it rather than that I disliked it.... I knew that if anything should happen to Mr. Makiguchi, there was no one but me to take over his post. But because of the feeling I have just described, I contrived somehow or other not to become president."

Toda had attempted to groom one or two other leaders as presidential candidates, but none lived up to his and Makiguchi's expectations. After the postwar reconstruction of the association, his fellow leaders asked Toda time and again to take over the presidency, but, he said, "I could not bring myself to it."

What changed his mind, he says, was the "ineffable" experience he had for the second time in his life—his business catastrophe—which he recognized as Nichiren's punishment. He became "convinced with my whole body that I must save the world from its agony."

Soka Gakkai's membership was then assessed at about three thousand families, organized into twelve chapters; the temples of Nichiren Shoshu numbered just over one hundred, with a total of two hundred priests and about eighty thousand parishioners.

At the general meeting of Soka Gakkai that inaugurated Toda as president, held at Josen-ji temple in Mukojima, Tokyo, on May 3, 1951, he told the 1,500-odd members: "I intend to convert 750,000 families before I die. If this is not achieved by the time of my death, don't hold a funeral service for me but throw my ashes into the sea off Shinagawa."

With this bold goal set by its grimly determined leader, Soka Gakkai embarked on a seven-year conversion campaign. Toda was well aware that his target seemed fantastic. Only a few weeks earlier, in March 1951, at a meeting of leaders, he had remarked ironically: "At this rate [ninety-five families per month], we can reach an enormous number in ten thousand years."

As president, Toda seems to have followed two key policies:

1) closer cooperation with the priests of Taiseki-ji and other temples of Nichiren Shoshu, which improved relations between Soka Gakkai and the clergy and identified Soka Gakkai more closely with Nichiren Shoshu; and 2) the reorganization of the society, designed to enable Soka Gakkai to carry out a vigorous proselytizing campaign.

The former policy was significant in that Toda had not always displayed the reverence and humble loyalty that might be expected of a lay believer toward the priests at Taiseki-ji. Addressing members of his organization, he would often speak of "bad priests," compared with whom Toda was a far better student of the canon of Nichiren Shoshu in both knowledge and conduct. Nor did he consider all priests of Nichiren Shoshu paragons of virtue. His and Makiguchi's wartime experience with the priesthood of Taiseki-ji led Toda to conclude that his faith, like Makiguchi's, was firmer than that of some of the priests.

Toda expressed his view of the clergy-laity relationship in Nichiren Shoshu in the address he gave on December 15, 1954, at a dedication service for a new Nichiren Shoshu temple built at Takasaki, Gumma Prefecture, with contributions by Soka Gakkai members. Toda told the assembly:

> It is our obligation to conduct *shakubuku* and serve the temple.[9] Now that we have a new temple here, I want you to take good care of it. You see to it that the priest here doesn't starve. . . . But you must not allow the priest to swagger. [Priests] have always had a bad habit. They have the bad habit of making use of parishioners as though the lay people were their retainers or servants. You must never allow this to happen in Takasaki. If the priests are officers, we are the soldiers. In the big war of *shakubuku*, the soldiers can't sit and watch when the officers don't move. They must move past the officers to fight. . . .

Toda felt particularly bitter toward one Taiseki-ji priest, Jimon Ogasawara, who had favored the merger of Nichiren Shoshu with Nichiren Shu at Minobu to conform with the government policy of unifying all Nichiren sects. Ogasawara also advocated the ecletic Shinto-Buddhist theology, according

---

[9] The "temple" is used here collectively to refer to the priesthood of Nichiren Shoshu in distinction from its lay adherents.

to which Buddhist deities were merely manifestations of the
true deities—those of Shinto.[10] Such had been the atmosphere
at Taiseki-ji when Makiguchi was called to the temple and
directed to moderate his outspokenness in the interest of good
relations between the temple and the authorities. Toda felt
that the priests, and Ogasawara in particular, were thereby
largely responsible for the government suppression of Soka
Kyoiku Gakkai and for Makiguchi's death in jail.

Toda never forgot this, nor did he forgive Ogasawara. On
the eve of April 28, 1952, when Taiseki-ji held a major service
to commemorate the founding of the Nichiren sect in 1253,
Toda visited the temple with four thousand members of his
Youth Division and assaulted Ogasawara. Toda felt justified in
doing so to avenge his late teacher and demanded an apology
from the octogenarian priest. When Ogasawara refused, the
young men, who included Ikeda, later president of Soka Gakkai,
mobbed him and carried him on their shoulders, tagging him
with a placard inscribed "Tanuki Bozu" (Raccoon Monk).[11]
Ogasawara was taken to Makiguchi's grave, where he was
forced to sign a statement of apology.

Recalling this incident in an interview with the author in
July 1956, Toda admitted hitting the priest "twice" and said
that this was the cause of the extremely unfavorable press
his organization then received—which labeled Soka Gakkai as
a "violent religion."[12]

Ogasawara filed a complaint with the authorities against
Soka Gakkai for assault and battery. In November 1952,
Nissho, the high priest of Taiseki-ji, reprimanded Toda for the
April 27 incident, and Toda responded with an apology printed
in *Seikyo Shimbun*, Soka Gakkai's organ. He promised that
Soka Gakkai would follow "the iron rule of absolute obedience
to the policy of the [Taiseki-ji] administration" and would

[10] What Ogasawara advocated may be said to be the reverse of the
traditional Buddhist theory of *honji suijaku* (essence versus appearance,
primary being versus secondary being, etc.). When applied to the Shinto-
Buddhist relationship, it means that Shinto deities are mere manifestations of the true beings: Buddhist deities. The implication is that Buddhism is superior to Shinto.

[11] The raccoon, in popular Japanese belief, is capable of bewitching
human beings. As an epithet, the word *tanuki* carries connotations of
deceit and despicableness.

[12] *Japan Times*, July 21, 1956.

continue to serve its interests. "In response to the high priest's admonition," he said, "we shall forget completely what happened in the past. . . . But if Mr. Ogasawara should take steps like those he took during the war . . . we will resolutely carry out a firm struggle to safeguard our canon. For the sin of having troubled the revered high priest, I am resolved to atone and apologize with the conversion of the entire nation. It goes without saying that members of the Youth Division follow me in this regard."

In a pamphlet issued in May 1955, Ogasawara similarly "repented" his "indiscretion in having had the unfortunate conflict with Soka Gakkai." Ikeda, who led the four thousand young men to mob Ogasawara, says now that the incident was an act of kindness because the old priest, made to realize his apostasy, was grateful to Toda and Soka Gakkai and died a happy man.

On May 12, 1951, Toda made a formal appeal to High Priest Nissho, through the priest at Josen-ji temple, for a *honzon* for Soka Gakkai. The petition read, in part:

> Ever since 1930, when our first president, Tsunesaburo Maki-guchi, founded Soka Gakkai, we have received the bountiful mercy of the Daigohonzon. We, men of kindred spirit, have dedicated ourselves to the cause of *kosen rufu* . . . but it will be a long time before we can attain the goal. . . . Today Asia is faced with a great turmoil,[13] and when we humbly consider the prophecy of our great founder Nichiren Daishonin, through his *Rissho Ankoku Ron* and other writings, [we believe that] now is the time for us to carry out a great *shakubuku* of the entire nation. We are therefore profoundly resolved to dedicate ourselves body and soul to the achievement of *kosen rufu* in reverent observance of the Buddha's will.
>
> We ask Your Excellency to understand our true sentiment and bestow upon us a *gohonzon*[14] for attaining our goal of *shakubuku*.

In response to this petition, High Priest Nissho presented Toda and other leaders of Soka Gakkai with a *honzon* on May 19 at Taiseki-ji. The sacred scroll, written by Nissho, is now kept at Soka Gakkai headquarters.

---

[13] By "great turmoil," Toda meant the Korean War, then in progress.
[14] The prefix *go* is an honorific, and *gohonzon* may be translated as "honorable *honzon*."

Relations between Soka Gakkai and Taiseki-ji were also improved by their agreement to publish Nichiren's writings, preserved through the centuries in original manuscript form. A new edition was urgently needed for the indoctrination of Soka Gakkai members, since existing editions contained errors, and even they were scarce because of the rising demand. Another compelling reason for publishing the new edition was that it required the editorial supervision and knowledge of Nichiko (1867–1957), the fifty-ninth-generation high priest of Taiseki-ji, who was, in 1951, already eighty-four years old. Nichiko had spent more than half a century in research on Nichiren and Nikko. Thus, under Nichiko's supervision, members of the Study Department of Soka Gakkai prepared the 1,702-page volume entitled *Shimpen Nichiren Daishonin Gosho Zenshu* (New Edition of the Complete Writings of Nichiren the Great Saint). This book, which places more emphasis on Nichiren's writings than on the Lotus Sutra, is now the supreme scripture of Nichiren Shoshu and Soka Gakkai.

THE ROLE OF THE YOUTH DIVISION

When Toda became president of the association, he carried out an organizational reform, creating such sections as the Youth Division, Women's Division, Planning Division, and the like. The most important was the Youth Division, consisting of the Young Men's and the Young Women's divisions, for it has since served as the prime mover of Soka Gakkai.

After the July 11, 1951, inaugural meeting of the Young Men's Division—consisting of 187 members organized into four *butai* (corps)—Toda made the following speech:

> I am certain that the next president of Soka Gakkai is among those of you who have assembled here today. I am convinced he is among you. *Kosen rufu* is a mission which I must accomplish. I want every one of you to realize the sacred position you have. The youth is the motive force for any revolution, as can be seen in the case of the Meiji Restoration. In Nichiren Daishonin's days, too, his followers were all young men.
>
> I want you young men to accomplish this great, holy mission. Our aim is not so small as to cover only Japan, but Nichi-

ren Daishonin has ordered us to spread the Lotus Sutra to Korea, China, and India. Today I take this opportunity to greet the person to be our next president and congratulate you with all my heart on the inauguration of this young men's group.

Among the young men was Ikeda, then twenty-four years old, destined to be the next president. Evidently Toda had by then determined by himself to whom he should hand over the presidency at his death or retirement. Members of the Youth Division of 1951 are the top leaders of Soka Gakkai and Komeito today. This group served as the spearhead of the great *shakubuku* march that earned Soka Gakkai both notoriety and an unparalleled increase in members.

The Young Women's Division, the other half of the Youth Division, was organized on July 19, 1951, with seventy members, composing five corps.

Toda organized and ran the Young Men's and Young Women's divisions as though they were military organizations, employing such terms as *butai* and *butaicho* (corps commander), and giving each corps a *butaiki* (corps standard). Another military-sounding unit was the *samboshitsu* (staff office), of which Ikeda was one of the initial members.

Neither his own experiences under Japan's military regime nor public reaction to his *modus operandi* bothered Toda. Military organization and discipline were made to serve his purpose because he thought them the most efficient. On the premise that "every religion other than Nichiren Shoshu is an evil religion," the young zealots attacked temples of other Buddhist sects, Christian churches, and headquarters of "new religions." They challenged their adversaries to debates, on the understanding that the loser write a statement of apology. Such apologies, collected in those years and kept by Soka Gakkai, testify to the "vigor" of the Youth Division in these early days.

However, the aggressive campaigning of Soka Gakkai youths, and their military organization, provided the press with excellent material for alarmist stories. Soka Gakkai was referred to as a "militarist religion," a "gangster religion," a "religion of violence," and suchlike. Press criticism reached its height in 1954. Soka Gakkai made headlines such as these in the major national dailies: "Violent Religion May See Bloodshed," "Youth in Gang Challenges by Argument," "Strange Menace in Religious World," "Education Ministry Conducts Nationwide Survey," and the like.[15]

In the same year, at the headquarters leaders' meeting of March 30, Toda created a new *samboshitsu* (staff office), with far-reaching consequences. Its chief, Daisaku Ikeda, explained its purpose:

> This office is to map out a long-range plan for *kosen rufu*. It is our urgent task to achieve *kosen rufu* in the next twenty-odd years. The time has come for us members of the Youth Division to carry out *kosen rufu* activities. This is the reason why the staff office has become necessary and been established.

Practically all the programs and plans for Soka Gakkai from that time on were mapped out by this office, headed by Ikeda.

Toda also appointed fifteen *butaicho* (corps commanders) for the Men's and Women's divisions respectively. On April 29, 1954, a general meeting of the Young Men's and Young Women's divisions was held, and *butaiki* (corps standards) were given to the component units. On May 9, the thirty corps, comprising 5,300 young men and women, displaying their unit flags, conducted a major parade through rains at Taiseki-ji. On October 31, also at Taiseki-ji, the men and women held a massive demonstration. The total membership of the two divisions had by that time increased to 10,390 (6,308 men and 4,082 women)—in less than three years since their inauguration.

After reviewing the columns of men and women, Toda, mounted on a white horse, addressed them:

> In our attempt at *kosen rufu,* we are without an ally. We must consider all religions our enemies, and we must destroy them. Ladies and gentlemen, it is obvious that the road ahead is full of obstacles. Therefore, you must worship the *gohonzon,* take the Soka Gakkai spirit to your heart, and cultivate the strength of youth. I expect you to rise to the occasion to meet the many challenges that lie ahead.

---

[15] Tokyo Daigaku Hoke-kyo Kenkyukai: *Nichiren Shoshu Soka Gakkai,* Sankibo Busshorin, Tokyo, 1962, p. 392.

The Importance of the Doctrine

Toda, rebuilding Soka Gakkai after the war, grounded his activities on regular lectures on the Lotus Sutra in an effort to provide the movement with a solid basis of doctrine. After he became president of Soka Gakkai in 1951, however, he replaced the lectures on the sutra with doctrinal studies by members on Nichiren's writings. Toda's successor, Ikeda, follows a similar policy of emphasis on Nichiren's writings. From May 1951, Toda lectured each Friday on the writings. At first his audience consisted of about fifty persons. In his last years, the lectures were held in the public hall of Toshima Ward of Tokyo, which, with a capacity of about two thousand, could not accommodate the regular audience.

Toda also established a hierarchy on the basis of doctrinal scholarship as another key program. As soon as he became president, he appointed twenty-four of his leading pupils as professors, assistant professors, lecturers, and assistants in the new Lecture Department. In September of the same year, the department was renamed the Study Department, and lectures were classified into five grades. Department members gave lectures to the local chapters throughout the country. They also edited *Shakubuku Kyoten* (Shakubuku Manual), the indispensable tool for conversion.[16]

Thus armed with both organization and doctrine, Soka Gakkai began the intensive *shakubuku* drive which, by the end of 1951, was credited with the conversion of 4,715 families, bringing total membership to 5,728 families, organized in twelve chapters.

For Soka Gakkai and all other Nichiren worshipers, the year 1952 held importance as the seven-hundredth anniversary (according to the traditional Japanese way of counting anniversaries) of the "establishment" of Nichiren's sect in 1253.

For Soka Gakkai, the significance of the year lay in the fact that the seven centuries after the establishment of the canon of Nichiren had seen the diffusion of the sacred phrase "Nammyoho Renge-kyo." In the new era to follow this period, *honzon* were to be propagated.

16 For further information on the Study Department, see page 144.

Through *shakubuku*, the membership of Soka Gakkai continued to snowball, and Toda's target of winning a membership of 750,000 families was achieved months before his death.

SHAKUBUKU: ITS MEANING AND METHOD

Soka Gakkai's intensive conversion method, *shakubuku*, has become identified in the public mind with Soka Gakkai itself. *Shakubuku*, however, is neither an invention nor a monopoly of Soka Gakkai or even Nichiren Shoshu. It is one of the two traditional Buddhist methods of conversion, the other being *shoju*. Buddhist sutras refer to them both, as did Nichiren in his writings. *Shakubuku*, literally meaning "break and subdue," is the forceful method of conversion, while *shoju* is the moderate, conciliatory approach. The former meant "breaking" the "wrong belief" of the person to be converted, even, according to a sutra called Nehan-gyo (Nirvana Sutra; in Sanskrit, Mahaparinibbanasuttanta), with the use of "the sword and bow and arrow." *Shoju*, on the other hand, meant gradual conversion through tentative acceptance of the "wrong belief" of the other party.

In *Kaimokusho*, Nichiren wrote that these two methods of conversion are "like fire and water" and must be used for distinctly different purposes. *Shoju* was to be employed when "the ignorant and the bad fill the land," while *shakubuku* was to be used when "the cunning or vicious" were numerous.

Nichiren advocated the use of *shakubuku* in his own time, because it was the age of *mappo* and Japan abounded in unscrupulous nihilists and criminals. He also felt that social reform could only be achieved through *shakubuku*—by steadfast opposition to entrenched authority.

Soka Gakkai claims that Nichiren's choice of the conversion method also applies to contemporary Japan, since it is "full of evil religions and their adherents."[17] *Shakubuku*, furthermore,

---

[17] Soka Gakkai Kyogakubu (Study Department, Soka Gakkai): *Nichiren Shoshu Kyogaku Kaisetsu* (Commentaries on Nichiren Shoshu Doctrine), Soka Gakkai, Tokyo, 1963, p. 245.

is "an act of austere love because it breaks the evil religion of the person who is *shakubuku*-ed and makes him commit himself to the correct faith. . . . It is like the love of a parent who sternly chides his child when he is bad. . . ."[18] Indeed, *shakubuku* is "absolutely an act of mercy," and this "mercy" must be that of "the stern father who, as an emissary of the Buddha, must love the common masses. Therefore he must relieve the person [to be *shakubuku*-ed] of agonies and show him his own ignorance of Buddhism. His attitude must be dignified, yet it must be full of infinite benevolence," according to *Shakubuku Kyoten*.[19]

Shakubuku Kyoten is designed to arm members of Soka Gakkai with all the doctrinal tools necessary for conversion. It summarizes the essential elements of Nichiren Shoshu, its differences from and "superiority" to other faiths and religions, and outlines Makiguchi's theory of value, offering also practical guidance on conversion techniques appropriate to a particular situation. It warns the reader that *shakubuku* is difficult, for to preach the teachings of Nichiren in the age of *mappo* necessarily means an endeavor under adverse circumstances.

"To attain Buddhahood means to live in eternal happiness. There is no greater happiness and higher value than this," argues the conversion manual. "The shortest road to attaining Buddhahood is *shakubuku*. If you conduct *shakubuku* with unshakable conviction, with no thought of what might happen to your own self, you will surely attain Buddhahood."

"When you conduct *shakubuku*, you will inevitably be spoken ill of, disliked, and hated," says *Shakubuku Kyoten*. But to encounter difficulties in the course of *shakubuku*, the reader is assured, means that his penalty for the wrongs committed in his previous incarnation is commuted.[20]

The objective of *kosen rufu* by *shakubuku* was set forth by Toda on May 3, 1951, in his inaugural address at Josen-ji temple as follows:

[18] Soka Gakkai Kyogakubu (Study Department, Soka Gakkai): *Bukkyo Tetsugaku Daijiten* (Encyclopedia of Buddhist Philosophy), Vol. 3 (1966), p. 477.
[19] Soka Gakkai Kyogakubu (Study Department, Soka Gakkai): *Shakubuku Kyoten* (Shakubuku Manual), Tokyo, 1967, p. 244.
[20] *Ibid.*, pp. 242–43.

There are some who think that *kosen rufu* would be achieved if we had the emperor accept a *gohonzon* and had him issue a rescript. This is an utterly foolish notion. *Kosen rufu* of today can be attained only when all of you take on evil religions and convert everyone in the country and let him accept a *gohonzon*. This is the only way we can establish the *hommon no kaidan*.

In his frequent addresses to his followers, Toda always stressed the earthly benefits they would receive from conducting *shakubuku*. On August 3, 1951, for instance, he told his audience: "You carry on *shakubuku* with conviction. If you don't do it now, let me tell you, you will never become happy." On September 1, 1954, he told an assembly of Soka Gakkai members:

> Let me tell you why you must conduct *shakubuku*. This is not to make Soka Gakkai larger but for you to become happier.
> . . . There are many people in this world who are suffering from poverty and disease. The only way to make them really happy is to *shakubuku* them. You might say it is sufficient for you to pray [to a *gohonzon*] at home, but unless you carry out *shakubuku* you will not receive any divine benefit. A believer [in Nichiren] who has forgotten *shakubuku* will receive no such benefit. . . .

With members thus impelled to carry out *shakubuku,* many of them inevitably went to extremes—pressuring potential converts into acquiescence.

These tactics not only made the press highly critical of Soka Gakkai; they also alarmed police and the Public Security Investigation Agency of the Ministry of Justice. On November 26, 1955, Goichiro Fujii, director of the agency, was quoted in a major national daily as saying that Soka Gakkai "was conducting a membership drive in a semi-gangster manner, using a military organization. . . . Depending on the outcome of our investigation, we might invoke the Anti-Subversive-Activities Law."

In response, Toda told a meeting of headquarters leaders on November 30 that he would not let this statement by Fujii go unchallenged. "This means that, without knowing facts, a government official made a foolish statement," he said. "The

Anti-Subversive-Activities Law is designed to control groups which try to destroy the state, the social order, and political life—the Communist Party, in particular. The spirit of the legislation was that it should not be invoked against anything else besides the Communist Party."

Soka Gakkai protested to Fujii for his alleged remark and was assured that the newspaper article "had no basis in fact" and that the official himself was very much troubled by the report. To Soka Gakkai, Fujii denied making such a statement and said that his agency was not investigating Soka Gakkai. The upshot was that the major daily totally retracted the article.

Nevertheless, Toda admitted in his November 30 address that Soka Gakkai members frequently went to extremes in the process of *hobobarai*, an essential step in conversion. A man who decides to join Nichiren Shoshu must remove all traces of other religions from own house—by burning Shinto and Buddhist images and tablets or anything related to Christianity. Even mandalas issued by Nichiren Shu temples must be removed. The convert is then taken to the local Nichiren Shoshu temple, where the priest conducts rites and endows him with a *gohonzon* to hang in the Buddhist altar at his home, before which he must pray daily and recite the *daimoku* (Nammyoho Renge-kyo).

Members of Soka Gakkai and their new converts often misunderstood the procedure of *hobobarai*, however. As a result, many converts destroyed, or were forced to destroy, even their ancestral tablets—often to the horror of the rest of their family, who were not sympathetic to Soka Gakkai or its practices.

Hobobarai aroused such popular criticism of Soka Gakkai that Toda advised leaders against going to the extreme of forcing new converts to burn their ancestral tablets or Shinto altars. In his November 30 address, he said it was not necessary to remove the shelf on which Shinto tablets were placed, only the tablets. Toda said, "You don't have to do it yourself. Tell the new convert, 'You do it yourself.' And if he says, 'Is it absolutely necessary?' you tell him, 'Yes, it is.' If he says, 'No, I can't destroy this—not this,' then it is better to leave him after saying, 'In that case, you think it over for half a year

or three months. When you come to the point where you can
get rid of that, then join our faith. Until then, you can't have
a *gohonzon*.' "

Toda told his audience not to offer to remove the convert's
Shinto tablets themselves. He cited the example of a member
who converted a housewife and made her remove these sacred
family objects without her husband's consent. A family quarrel
followed, and the husband in anger burned the *gohonzon*. "If
this should happen, it would be defeating the purpose of
shakubuku," Toda said.

However, the ruling that a new convert must remove the
relics of "evil religions" is firm. An official Soka Gakkai
publication put it this way: "Is it not permissible to keep
sacred objects and tablets of other religions without burning
them as long as one does not worship them?" The answer is:
"Nichiren Daishonin pointed out that the cause of unhappiness is evil religion. Wanting to keep relics of other religions
on the pretext that you don't worship them indicates your
attachment to evil religions. Then you can't say your faith is
unadulterated. There are cases of people who mistakenly
thought they had disposed of tablets and talismans of evil
religions. Because these objects remained in their houses,
however, these people suffered severe divine punishment. . . .
If you decide to join our faith after realizing that Nichiren
Shoshu is correct and that all other religions are evil, then
it is natural for you to carry out *hobobarai*."[21]

In the heyday of the *shakubuku* drive, there were clearly
many cases of extremism through genuine misunderstanding
on the part of overzealous members of the lower ranks of
Soka Gakkai. But such excesses should not be identified with
Toda himself nor with Soka Gakkai's official policy on *shakubuku*, for Soka Gakkai leaders did stress the need for
moderation and reasonableness.

THE PROMISE OF SECULAR BENEFITS

It seems unlikely that Soka Gakkai's intensive conversion
campaign could have won so many converts so quickly simply

---

[21] Kodaira, *op. cit.*, p. 140.

through members' proclaiming their conviction that Nichiren Shoshu was the one truth faith. The secular benefits Soka Gakkai promised potential converts undoubtedly account for its dynamic appeal. The line of reasoning presented was simple enough: if you are unhappy about anything—your poor health or financial condition—the key to happiness is simply to place your faith in the Daigohonzon, the sacred tablet inscribed by Nichiren. For that, one has only to join Soka Gakkai.

In his June 5, 1955, address, Toda likened the Daigohonzon to a "machine which produces happiness." He elaborated:

> Suppose a machine which never fails to make everyone happy were built by the power of science or by medicine. . . . Such a machine, I think, could be sold at a very high price. Don't you agree? If you used it wisely, you could be sure to become happy and build up a terrific company. You could make a lot of money. You could sell such machines for about ¥100,000 apiece.
>
> But Western science has not yet produced such a machine. It cannot be made. Still, such a machine has been in existence in this country, Japan, since seven hundred years ago. This is the Daigohonzon. [Nichiren] Daishonin made this machine for us and gave it to us common people. He told us: "Use [the machine] freely. It won't cost you any money." And yet, people of today don't want to use it because they don't understand the explanation that the Daigohonzon is such a splendid machine.

Toda explained that some people suffer from poverty and others from disease because of *karma* (destiny—the consequences of what one does in one reincarnation or the next). Someone is poor today because in his previous life he performed the deeds that would make him poor in his current life. Unless a person made proper preparation in his current life, he would not be reborn into a life of affluence.

Toda's materialist view of the benefits to be gained from worshiping Nichiren's mandala is typified in the following excerpt from an address he made in 1953 in Sendai:

> When I meet you, I don't ask: "Are you keeping faith?" The reason is that I take your *shakubuku* for granted. What I really want to ask you is how your business is, whether you are making money, and if you are healthy. Only when all of

you receive divine benefit do I feel happy. A person who says "I keep faith; I conduct *shakubuku*" when he is poor—I don't consider him my pupil. Your faith has only one purpose: to improve your business and family life. Those who talk about "faith" and do not attend to their business are sacrilegious. Business is a service to the community. I will expel those of you who do nothing but *shakubuku* without engaging in business.

Here Toda expressed the personal philosophy that had guided his actions before he became a full-time leader of Soka Gakkai. He had a strong faith in Nichiren, but at the same time he was a dedicated businessman, intent on acquiring material wealth.

Later in the same year, at the November 22 general meeting of Soka Gakkai, Toda said:

How can we live happily in this world and enjoy life? If anyone says he enjoys life without being rich and even when he is sick—he is a liar. We've got to have money and physical vigor, and underneath all we need life force. This we cannot get by theorizing or mere efforts as such. You can't get it unless you worship a *gohonzon*. . . . It may be irreverent to use this figure of speech, but a *gohonzon* is a machine that makes you happy. How to use this machine? You conduct five sittings of prayer in the morning and three sittings in the evening and *shakubuku* ten people. Let's make money and build health and enjoy life to our hearts' content before we die!

Toda's worldly values and down-to-earth language are again characteristically expressed in the speech he gave on August 3, 1955, at a meeting of the Niigata chapter of Soka Gakkai. It is reproduced here almost in its entirety:

When I view the situation in this world, I find rich people and I find poor people. There are families in which man and wife live happily together; in others there are always quarrels. There are homes in which the members all enjoy good health and a happy life. There are homes full of sick people. There are healthy people, and there are unhealthy people. Why is this?

No Occidental philosophy has been able to account for this. It has been explained only by the Buddhist philosophy of the Orient. Its conclusion is that our life is eternal and that we may die in this world, but we must be reborn in this world again. Just as a man who lived yesterday lives today too, a person who lives in his present life will have to be reborn. Just as we must recognize the existence of our next life, we must recognize our past life. This is the basis of the Oriental Buddhist philosophy. Whether you know it or not, it is the fact of life.

Therefore a person who is healthy today gave cause in his past life for his present good health. A person who is rich today gave cause for it in his past life. This is the Buddhist explanation of the fact that there are people who are noble and humble, rich and poor, happy and unhappy. If any one of you here is poor or suffering because of lack of money, it means that you, according to Buddhism, were a burglar in your past life. I think there may be many ex-burglars here now. "Not me. It must be my neighbor," you might say. But then you tell yourself there isn't much you can do about this life. But you can be a rich man in your next life and have a good husband or have a good child.

For that, you must do good deeds now to make sure that your next life will be what you want. This is the basis of Buddhist theory.

But just think for a moment. Everyone wants to overcome his destiny. A poor man, no matter how foolish, would not think he should be content with his status. A sick man would not say he is content with being sick. He wants to be cured; he wants to be healthy. A poor man wants to be a rich man. This is quite natural. Yet the law preached by the Buddha is inexorable.

It holds that you cannot change your life now; you must wait until your next reincarnation. This is a problem indeed, isn't it? But if this is the only solution Buddhism can offer, then I would not like to be a Buddhist. No, thanks. Because I couldn't tell if I could have it my way in my next life.

But the Buddhist law of [Nichiren Daishonin] is better than that of the Buddha. That's the reason why we shout: "We are not pupils of the Buddha. Buddha's law is of no use. It's got to be Daishonin's Buddhist law." Daishonin said: "I am making a thing called a *gohonzon*. If you recite 'Nam-myoho Renge-kyo' in front of this *gohonzon*, I will endow you with the condition you failed to create in your past life, enabling you to overcome your destiny instantly." This is a wonderful thing for which we must be grateful. . . .

If there is a poor man among you, all you must do is to believe in this *gohonzon* and carry out *shakubuku* in earnest. Then you will begin to have the good luck with which you did not come into this world. . . .

When I hold a question-and-answer session at Taiseki-ji, I hear many questions. The two simplest ones are how a poor man can become rich and how a man suffering from tuberculosis can be cured. A man in the primary stage of tuberculosis can definitely be cured. I think there are many people who want to have a lot of money. But they can't get money by wishing, I think. I want you to become rich by having a firm faith in a *gohonzon*. How about it? Do you mind that?

Suppose the Tokyo University Hospital invented a medicine that would be sure to make you rich if only you had it injected into you between the hours of six and seven in the morning. I am sure everyone would get up early in the morning and go to the hospital. And they would get the shots even though they might have to wait for one or two hours. And if the medicine was so effective that if you continued to take it for one year you would make hundreds of thousands of yen, and if you continued this for two years you would make millions of yen, and for three years so many more millions of yen, and if a doctor could really do this, then I think there would be a long line of people in front of his clinic. You too would go there, I am sure.

Now, you can get the same result without having to go to the Tokyo University Hospital but by sitting in your own home for only thirty minutes in the morning. You don't have to spend a single yen for train or tram fare. The only thing you would need would be candles and incense sticks. Isn't this a cheap investment? People who don't do this, I say, are fools. Do it in the morning and in the evening. Don't ever doubt the *gohonzon*. Keep faith. If you doubt, it will be no good. . . .

If you do as I tell you, and if things don't work out as you want by the time I come to Niigata next time, then you may come up here and beat me and kick me as much as you want. With this promise, I conclude my talk for tonight.

Toda's repeated references to "the poor and the sick" make it clear that his conversion campaign was aimed primarily at such people. And evidently, for many of them, their new faith worked. Indeed, a surprisingly large number of Soka Gakkai's top-ranking leaders today are people who joined the association when they were ill with tuberculosis and who subsequently regained their health. President Ikeda himself is one of them. For years, before and after joining Soka Gakkai, he was an invalid. The exceedingly heavy schedule he carries today would be a menace to the health of any man. "Only my spirit keeps me going," he has told the author.

Soka Gakkai's daily, *Seikyo Shimbun,* constantly carries reports of members cured of serious diseases, including even cancer, through their faith in *gohonzon.* One ground for criticism of Soka Gakkai in the early years of *shakubuku* was its alleged claim to faith healing. But in an interview with the author in July 1956, Toda, asked to comment on the claim, burst out: "That's preposterous. We tell people to see doctors when they are sick." He added, however: "We will cure those cases which the doctors can't. Suppose you have a polio victim. If modern medicine can't make him walk, bring him here. I will cure him."

Toda also confirmed a press report on one case of attempted resurrection by prayer in northern Japan. A five-year-old child died of an unknown cause. The doctor concerned reported the case to the police, who wanted to conduct an autopsy. But the parents, who were members of Soka Gakkai, refused for five days to surrender the child's body, while praying for his revival.

"You can't blame the parents," Toda explained. "No one likes to have his child's body cut up. Besides, it is sometimes possible to revive the dead with prayer."[22]

THE CHARGE OF THEOCRACY

Another chief cause of criticism of Soka Gakkai during Toda's *shakubuku* era, and even in the early years of Ikeda's leadership, was its plan to establish a state-built sanctuary *(kokuritsu no kaidan)* when the aim of *kosen rufu* was achieved. Toda himself and Soka Gakkai's official publications declared this to be the supreme aim of Soka Gakkai. Nichiren Shoshu theology holds that the erection of the *kaidan* was the only task left unfinished by Nichiren. Upon completion of *kosen*

22 *Japan Times,* July 21, 1956.

rufu, the Daigohonzon, now kept in Taiseki-ji's *hoanden* (sanctuary), is to be enshrined in the *kaidan* for all converts to worship. According to Toda, this would be *obutsu myogo*— that is, a harmonious blending of government and Buddhism.

This theory is drawn from Nichiren's own conviction and writings—in particular, the passage in *Sandai Hihosho* referred to in Chapter 4. Indeed, Soka Gakkai claims that its aim in participating in politics is to achieve *obutsu myogo*. Toda said that when *obutsu myogo* was accomplished, which would be simultaneous with *kosen rufu*, the *kokuritsu no kaidan* was to be erected by the contemporary counterpart of what Nichiren referred to as *chokusen* (imperial decree) and *migyosho* (shogunate order). According to Soka Gakkai, this would be a resolution or law passed by the Diet through constitutional procedures—that is, by the "total will of the people."

In his thesis *Obutsu Myogo Ron*, serialized in the theoretical organ *Daibyakurenge* from August 1956, Toda wrote:

> We are interested in politics because of the need to achieve *kosen rufu*, spreading of the sacred phrase of "Nam-myoho Renge-kyo," one of the Three Great Secret Laws. In other words, the only purpose of our going into politics is the erection of the *hommon no kaidan*. We believe that the precept of *kaidan* stated in *Sandai Hiho Bonjoji* [*Sandai Hihosho*] is the supreme mandate of Nichiren Daishonin.[23]

He did caution his followers, however, not to imagine that such a goal may be attained through the conversion of the ruler, leading automatically to the conversion of all his subjects, as happened before in Japanese history or as Nichiren might have anticipated. Toda saw that modern democracy and the political consciousness of the people made such a notion unfeasible.[24] But he did look forward to the day when the entire nation of Japan, including the emperor, was converted to Nichiren Shoshu. Toda often referred to the mandala *(honzon)* by Nichiren intended for the emperor of Japan, once he had become a votary of the Lotus Sutra, which was to be hung in the Shishinden (also called Shishiiden) in the Kyoto Imperial Palace. Known as Shishinden no Honzon

---

[23] Quoted by Kodaira, *op. cit.*, p. 166.
[24] See page 104.

and believed to have been inscribed by Nichiren in 1280, this particular *honzon* is still kept at Taiseki-ji. It is exhibited annually on April 6 and 7, in the airing rite called *omushibarai* (driving away bookworms). Toda repeatedly mentioned the presence of the Shishinden no Honzon at Taiseki-ji as evidence of the "absolute superiority" of Nichiren Shoshu over all other religions and sects.[25]

On the relationship between the state and the propagation of his own faith, Toda told a chapter of Soka Gakkai on March 27, 1955:

> When *kosen rufu* is completed or in the process of being carried out, everyone, be he in business, journalism, the film world, or government—whether he is a business executive or a janitor— everyone realizes the worth of *gohonzon*. There will be Diet members from among these people, and there will be a petition for building the *hommon no kaidan,* and it will be approved by the Diet, and then the emperor will realize the great divine benefit of the *gohonzon*. Then *kosen rufu* will have been achieved.[26]

Other Soka Gakkai leaders also spoke of building the "national hall of worship" to symbolize the attainment of their goal. For instance, Yoshihei Kodaira, head of the organization's Study Department, wrote that such a national sanctuary "is to be built upon completion of *kosen rufu* with the total will of the Japanese nation."[27]

Such statements by Soka Gakkai leaders created the popular impression that Soka Gakkai aimed at dominating the national legislature and establishing a national hall of worship by and with the prerogatives of the emperor. This gave rise to fears that Soka Gakkai's ultimate objective was the establishment of a theocracy—that it planned to impose its own religion on the

[25] Toda proudly referred to this *honzon* reserved for the emperor, almost continuously in his addresses of September 19 and 30, October 9 and 18, 1954. Josei Toda: *Toda Josei Zenshu* (Complete Works of Josei Toda), Vol. 2, Wakosha, Tokyo, 1965, pp. 268–80.

[26] One member of the imperial family is known to have espoused the faith of Nichiren Shoshu. Empress Teimei (1894–1951), consort of Emperor Taisho and mother of the present emperor, was given a *honzon* by Nikkyo (1869–1945), the sixty-second-generation high priest of Taiseki-ji, in 1941. (Soka Gakkai Kyogakubu: *Bukkyo Tetsugaku Daijiten*, Vol. 4, p. 1019.) Toda referred to this relatively little-known fact in his address of December 23, 1953, saying that the empress dowager received the *honzon* "secretly."

[27] Kodaira, *op. cit.*, p. 165.

entire nation—which the constitution of Japan specifically proscribes. In response to public criticism, Soka Gakkai was to alter its policy and pronouncements under Ikeda's leadership. This will be dealt with in Chapter 7.

Despite the fears and ill feeling it generated in the public mind, Soka Gakkai continued to expand under Toda's leadership. On December 25, 1957, it announced that the target of 750,000 member families, set by Toda in 1951, had already been achieved. Membership figures for each year from 1951 to 1957 were given as follows:

Year	Number of Member Families
1951	5,728
1952	22,324
1953	70,000
1954	164,272
1955	307,490
1956	500,000
1957	750,000

Toda's Last Days

On March 1, 1958, Soka Gakkai dedicated the Daikodo (Grand Lecture Hall) at Taiseki-ji. The building, which cost about ¥400,000,000 (well over $1,000,000) and took fifteen months to build, was the first of many built by Soka Gakkai for Taiseki-ji. The lecture hall of a temple is traditionally a place where priests study the canon of their religion. It dates back to the days of the Buddha, when he taught his pupils in an enclosure that usually had no roof.

For the March 1 celebration, Toda invited Prime Minister Nobusuke Kishi, who, although he himself did not attend, sent a proxy to present his congratulatory message. A cabinet member who was invited also had his message read by a proxy. Toda was apparently most anxious to have the prime minister of Japan visit Taiseki-ji for the prestige it would have lent his organization, which then still carried a social stigma. He must also have wanted to vaunt the million-dollar building his organization had contributed to the temple, which was, for Toda, a tangible symbol of his lifelong dedication to Nichiren Shoshu.

For a second time, Toda invited Kishi to visit Taiseki-ji—on Sunday, March 16—and the prime minister accepted. Toda lined up six thousand members of the Young Men's and Young Women's divisions at the temple to welcome the prime minister and to present an elaborate program for him. But Kishi again failed to come and sent on his behalf a former member of his cabinet, his wife, daughter, and son-in-law.

To celebrate the completion of the Grand Lecture Hall, 200,000 Soka Gakkai members visited Taiseki-ji in the month of March, throughout which Toda remained at the temple to supervise the pilgrimages. In the meantime, he became seriously ill, and he left Taiseki-ji on April 1 to be taken immediately to the Nihon University Hospital at Tokyo's Surugadai, where he died on the evening of the following day.

On April 4, a newspaper ran an obituary stating that Toda had died of cardiac weakness. The same paper on the following day carried an announcement by Soka Gakkai, stating that Josei Toda, its president, had died at 6:30 p.m. on April 2, after "fulfilling all his wishes."[28]

The exact nature of Toda's fatal illness has never been officially disclosed by Soka Gakkai. But Toda himself gave a clue in what was probably his last article, dated February 14, 1958, in an official periodical. In it he said that his health had deteriorated in April 1957, and on November 20 his liver condition became critical. "Every doctor looked as though he thought there was no hope for me," he wrote. But he recovered sufficiently to visit Taiseki-ji in January 1958, and a checkup on January 7, he wrote, showed that "my liver trouble was completely cured." He still suffered, however, from the diabetes that he had developed in prison fifteen years before. The cell life in jail had broken his health. He also had trouble with his pancreas, which was supposedly responsible for the damage caused to his left eye.

Toda called his health *sansho shima* (three obstacles and four devils) : a test of faith, according to traditional Buddhist

28 Tadakuni Nakaba: *Nippon no Choryu* (The Current of Japan), Yuki Shobo, Tokyo, 1968, p. 96.

belief. The firmer the faith, the more challenging the test is supposed to be.

Funeral services for Toda were held at Jozai-ji temple in Ikebukuro, Tokyo, where, thirty years before, he had been admitted to the faith of Nichiren Shoshu. About 120 persons attended.

An official Soka Gakkai funeral for Toda was held on April 20 at Tokyo's Aoyama Funeral Hall, attended by 250,000 members of Soka Gakkai from all over Japan and abroad. Among the attendants who offered incense at the altar for the deceased was Prime Minister Nobusuke Kishi.

Toda's chief pupil and successor, Daisaku Ikeda, gives some insight into Toda's personal magnetism and leadership qualities:

> The charm of Josei Toda as a man was unique. Upon meeting him for the first time, every new member, even though he did not understand anything about religion, was attracted to Toda by his personal charm. Toda's charm left a lasting impression on everyone with whom he came into contact. Toda did not consciously manipulate human beings. If anything, the opposite was the case. He had no deliberate plans. He was open-hearted, and he did not discriminate. Toda did not discriminate between rich and poor, noble and humble. Whether it was a middle-aged laborer, panting under the burden of making a living somehow, or a woman bemoaning the philandering of her rich black-marketing husband, it did not matter. There was none more sympathetic with the sorrows of each person's destiny than Toda. To him, everyone's problem was his own. Because he could not ignore unhappiness, he taught people to realize the rigors of one's three incarnations [past, present, and future], preached the infinite divine benefit of the *gohonzon*, and stirred in each man a faith that lifted him out of despair. . . .
>
> He was tolerant with anyone who would confess to a criminal record. But he did not tolerate anyone who responded to his guidance—on which he staked his own life—with vanity, sycophancy, adulation, and arrogance. He would suddenly fly into a fiery rage, and with all his might he would destroy that vanity and arrogance. He never allowed himself an insincere, sly compromise. . . .
>
> Many people found it difficult to understand such a sudden

change in his mood. This is perhaps because they did not realize the working of Toda's mind, which was able to sniff out mendacity more sensitively than the mind of anyone else.

Those persons who wondered why he became so angry over such a trifle often realized the reason later—and realized that Toda's fury was justified—when they saw what happened to the persons Toda had rebuked. Usually these people were astonished to find that Toda's seeming fury had its roots in his deep love.[29]

[29] Daisaku Ikeda: *Ningen Kakumei* (The Human Revolution), Vol. 3, Seikyo Shimbun-sha, Tokyo, 1967, pp. 88–90.

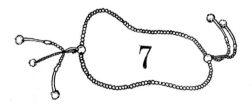

7

Ikeda and His Leadership

Soka Gakkai After Toda's Death

Soka Gakkai's critics and rivals expected the organization to disintegrate or fragment after Toda's premature death at the age of fifty-eight. Because Soka Gakkai was so closely identified with Toda, it was difficult for outsiders to foresee the emergence of another such leader from among his followers.

On May 3, 1958, one month after Toda's death, Soka Gakkai held its eighteenth convention at Tokyo's Ryogoku. Over the platform hung a portrait of the late Toda and a banner carrying the slogan "Danketsu" (unity or solidarity) to signify the resolve of the organization to maintain its cohesion. Among the speakers was Daisaku Ikeda, then chief of staff of the Youth Division, who exhorted the assembly to "smash whatever may stand in the way of our march toward the realization of *kosen rufu.*"

In June of the same year, Ikeda was appointed general director, which put him virtually in charge of the entire organization. He did not become president, however, until two years later, on May 3, 1960, at the general meeting. President Ikeda opened his inaugural address with the following remarks:

> Though I am still young, on behalf of the pupils of the late Mr. Toda, let me take the command of the organization for a step forward toward *kosen rufu* for the establishment of the *hommon no kaidan.* Needless to say, Soka Gakkai is an organization of adherents of Nichiren Shoshu. Therefore the basic spirit of our society is to devote ourselves to the Daigohonzon and serve His Excellency the High Priest.

In accordance with the spirit of our first president, Mr. Tsunesaburo Makiguchi, and the second president, our teacher, Josei Toda, who had loyally dedicated themselves to the head temple, I, representing the entire membership of our organization, pledge even greater loyalty to His Excellency. Soka Gakkai is the greatest ally of the masses. Our enemies are the evil religions. Evil religions drive people to hell. True Buddhism makes Buddhas out of all people. Nichiren Daishonin said the source of all unhappiness and misfortunes of people is evil religions. It was our teacher, Mr. Josei Toda, who repeated this great saying.

With the great spirit of this teacher of ours for destroying the evil religions, we, his pupils, must once again fiercely attack them.

Ikeda made two things clear: that Soka Gakkai, as a lay association, was subordinate to the church, Taiseki-ji, and that he would pursue his predecessor's policy of "destroying other religions."

Ikeda set a new goal for *shakubuku:* three million families in seven years—a figure based, Ikeda said, on a remark Toda had made on February 10, 1958, in private conversation with him. The new president urged the assembly to "carry on *shakubuku* to win three million families before the seventh anniversary of the death of our teacher, Mr. Josei Toda."

Another goal Ikeda set was the building of the Daikyakuden (Grand Reception Hall) within the same time limit—to be dedicated by Soka Gakkai to Taiseki-ji. This too was in accordance with the wishes of Toda, who had told his close disciples: "Build a Daikyakuden at the temple by using products of all the countries of the world."

IKEDA'S BACKGROUND

Daisaku Ikeda was born on January 2, 1928, the fifth son of Nenokichi Ikeda of Omori, Tokyo, who made and sold dried seaweed *(nori)*. The senior Ikeda had difficulty supporting his family of seven sons and two daughters, partly because his livelihood was at the mercy of too many variable conditions, especially weather.

Daisaku was a frail child during his primary-school days.

When his father could not afford to send him to secondary school the boy went to higher primary school, a tuition-free public school. In 1942, he entered a private commercial high school called the Toyo Shogyo. It was a time when all school children had to spend more time working in munitions factories than in the classroom. Ikeda was stricken with tuberculosis and pleurisy.

How a youth in poor health, doubtful of his own future in the uncertain postwar era, found a cause to which to dedicate himself, Ikeda described in *Ningen Kakumei*, in which the portions dealing with Shin'ichi Yamamoto and his encounter and life with Toda are thinly veiled autobiography.

After finishing commercial high school, Ikeda worked in a factory in Kamata, Tokyo. A sensitive lad with a literary bent, he privately organized a group of young men to study literature, art, politics, economics, and philosophy. His was but one of innumerable similar groups formed throughout Japan in those topsy-turvy postwar years when young men and women groped for new values. Their appearance throughout the country was also a product of the need felt by young people to fill the intellectual hiatus left by their skimpy wartime schooling.

The members of Ikeda's group, called Kyoyukai, sought to extend their knowledge in all fields through discussion meetings. They came from all walks of life: students, engineers, factory hands, civil servants—all between twenty and thirty years of age. One night they would discuss Dante and the Renaissance. On another, a member would read a paper on inflation in Weimar Germany by way of warning against the aggravating inflation in Japan at that time. On other occasions, democracy, communism, and the emperor system were subjects of discussion.

During these months of doubt and questioning, Ikeda met Toda for the first time when a member of the Kyoyukai, a young woman who had been at primary school with Ikeda, invited him to a lecture given by Toda at her home. Her family had earlier been converted to Nichiren Shoshu through the Soka Gakkai drive. "There is a lecture on philosophy at my home on the night of the fourteenth," she told Ikeda. "Won't you come? It is philosophy of life."

"Bergson?" Ikeda queried. "Who is the lecturer?"

"A man named Mr. Josei Toda. He is terrific. You should come."

Ikeda had never heard of a philosopher by that name, but he decided to attend. When he arrived, Toda was lecturing on Nichiren's *Rissho Ankoku Ron.* Afterwards, Ikeda was introduced to Toda, whose sincerity impressed the young visitor, although he found Toda's explanation of his Buddhist philosophy incomprehensible.

Most other leaders of Soka Gakkai were also present and all waited to see whether the newcomer would accept the Nichiren Shoshu faith on the spot and join Soka Gakkai. But Ikeda told Toda he would think it over. He recalled later that he had felt that conversion was like "being bound up or traveling to a strange world—into darkness." Yet he could not deny that "the encounter with Toda had an impact on his mind."

On August 24, 1947, Ikeda, accompanied by two leaders of Soka Gakkai who had been at the August 14 meeting, formally joined the association by going through the rites at the Kankiryo (since renamed as Shorin-ji) in Nakano, Tokyo. The priest who administered the rites for Ikeda was Taiei Horigome, who later became Nichijun, the sixty-fifth-generation high priest at Taiseki-ji.

This first encounter with Ikeda, a nineteen-year-old youth, left a deep impression on Toda—then forty-eight years old—because it reminded Toda of his first meeting with Makiguchi, when he had been nineteen and Makiguchi forty-eight.

Like most other Soka Gakkai members, Ikeda had no clear idea of what he was joining. "His face registered complicated feelings," Ikeda said of Shin'ichi Yamamoto in *Ningen Kakumei.* "Because he was a man who thought about things earnestly, he was concerned about his own health. His health was not at all good. Rather, he had to struggle against disease from day to day. It is clear that he himself did not know if he would devote his whole life to the practice of Buddhism and to a religious reformation."

Although Ikeda joined Soka Gakkai and attended lectures and discussion meetings of the association from time to time, he was still suffering from poor health and the rigors of a working man's life in postwar Japan. He worked in the office of a printing shop at Shimbashi during the day and spent whatever spare time he had reading.

Nor did Ikeda have an opportunity for a further meeting with Toda. In the autumn of 1948, however, Ikeda accepted a job at Toda's publishing office, and after giving his current employer notice he began working for Toda's Nihon Shogakkan at Nishi Kanda in January 1949. One of his assignments was to edit the magazine for boys, *Boken Shonen*, but the magazine folded up after three months, when Toda's business failed.

By mid-1949, Ikeda was leading a relatively stable life, attending evening classes at Taisei Gakuin, a private school.[1] But Toda's business venture was in critical condition, and Ikeda shared all the difficulties with his teacher Toda. Then Ikeda had to give up night school, partly because of his ill health and partly at Toda's insistence. Ikeda hoped that Toda would let him attend a better-known university when he had recovered his health. Knowing that he had frustrated Ikeda's desire to study, Toda offered to be his private tutor. "Leave your education up to me," he told Ikeda and began to teach his young protégé, every Sunday, such subjects as government, economics, law, classic Chinese, chemistry, and other sciences—though no Western languages. Ikeda attributes the existence of today's Soka Gakkai to the close teacher-pupil relationship that was built in these months from the beginning of 1950 to early 1951.

When Toda assumed that the failure of his business venture was a divine punishment and decided to devote all his time and energy to religious activities as head of Soka Gakkai, Ikeda followed him as a member of the Youth Division. In May, 1952, Ikeda married Kaneko Shiraki, a member of Soka Gakkai, whose father had been a Nichiren Shoshu adherent since before the war. The Todas acted as official go-betweens at the wedding ceremony.

As a member of the Youth Division, Ikeda came to be known as a fearless and eminently successful campaigner, and his

---

[1] Taisei Gakuin admitted students regardless of their educational backgrounds and educated them according to its founder-principal's unique educational ideal. In 1951, it became an accredited junior college called Fuji Tanki Daigaku.

prestige among his fellow members rose rapidly. In March 1954 he was appointed chief of staff of the division.

Like the first two presidents of Soka Gakkai, Ikeda, who was to become the third president, experienced life in police custody and interrogation by public prosecutors. In the 1957 Osaka by-election for the House of Councilors, Soka Gakkai ran a candidate. During the campaign, Ikeda and another leader were arrested on charges of having directed unlawful campaign tactics. It was charged that some Tokyo members of Soka Gakkai had come to Osaka to distribute cash among voters by inserting ¥100 notes in cigarette packs. Ikeda was arrested on July 3, 1957, and released on July 17. His trial began in September and continued until January 1962, when the court acquitted him.

Characteristically, Soka Gakkai treated the affair as an instance of government suppression and, through its organ *Seikyo Shimbun*, urged members to strengthen their faith and to resolve to withstand official repression.

President Toda himself, however, told a meeting of Osaka members on July 17, the day of Ikeda's release, that when he had heard about the election law violation charge, he thought that Socialists or Communists were responsible. "But on checking up, I found it was our own members," he said. Toda regarded any attempt to bribe voters with cash as an unthinkable campaign method for Soka Gakkai to use, and the organization expelled the individuals concerned. The particular candidate, Tatsuyoshi Nakao, lost the by-election but was successful in the 1959 House of Councilors election.

Ikeda's brush with the law raised his stature as a leader of Soka Gakkai in the eyes of President Toda. It also helped to strengthen Ikeda's self-confidence, undoubtedly preparing him for the topmost position in the organization.

In Soka Gakkai, no one is elected by vote, and Ikeda's appointment as president was a foregone conclusion. In 1951, Toda had said that he would hand over the presidency to a member of the Young Men's Division, not to a fellow pupil of Makiguchi, all of whose pupils except Toda had backslid under wartime suppression.

On February 17, 1952, Toda had declared: "I will give the post of third president to the Youth Division, not to anyone among the pupils of Mr. Makiguchi. The reason is that [Makiguchi's pupils] are old men. There will, of course, be only one president to whom I will hand over this organization. But when that happens, I shall not tolerate any split. Just as Makiguchi's pupils today support me, I want Toda's pupils to support the third president. . . ."

The wisdom of Toda's choice of successor was demonstrated more than anything else by the spectacular increase in Soka Gakkai membership under Ikeda. At the end of 1958, the year Toda died, the membership was announced to be 1,050,000 families; at the end of 1959, it was reported to be 1,300,000, multiplying to 6,240,000 by May 1967.

Ikeda's qualifications for the presidency had shown themselves early. The Kamata chapter, of which he was a leader, had been able to convert only thirty or forty families a month—at the most, ninety-odd. In early 1952, the head of the chapter talked to Ikeda, and they resolved to convert two hundred families in February 1952, a target achieved largely because of Ikeda. This is the basis of a tradition in Soka Gakkai that February is the month of *shakubuku*.

In July 1956, Soka Gakkai ran six candidates from its Culture Bureau in the House of Councilors election. Three were successful, including one from Osaka—Giichiro Shiraki, then head of the Osaka chapter. Soka Gakkai membership in the Osaka area at that time numbered barely 30,000 families, but Shiraki garnered a total of 210,000 votes, placing at the top of all candidates from the same constituency. No doubt Shiraki's popularity as an ace professional baseball pitcher assisted his success. But Soka Gakkai points out that his election would not have been possible had not Ikeda carefully cultivated the Osaka constituency for a year and a half in advance.

The Modification of Goals

Under Ikeda's leadership, Soka Gakkai members, particularly those of the Youth Division, often challenged leaders of established religions and "new religions" to public debate. The press maintained its criticism of Soka Gakkai's high-pressure proselytizing, while Soka Gakkai reacted with strong protests against the mass media's "distortion" of facts and "failure to understand" the association.[2]

In the meantime, with a new president came changes in the structure and the pattern of activities of the association. On May 3, 1951, his first anniversary as president, Ikeda transformed the Culture Department into the Culture Bureau, incorporating the newly created Economics, Politics, Education, and Speech departments. In December of the same year, the Art Department was added.

This Culture Bureau represented the nonreligious sphere of Soka Gakkai's activities, of which politics was the major element. In retrospect, it is evident that the creation of the new bureau, with its Political Department, was the first step toward Soka Gakkai's full-fledged participation in the nation's politics.

One tangible result of the increase in membership under Ikeda is the Daikyakuden (Grand Reception Hall), which Soka Gakkai built and dedicated to Taiseki-ji in 1964. A *kyakuden*, according to Nichiren Shoshu tradition, is a hall where *kyaku* (guests)—that is, worshipers—come before a *gohonzon*, the object of worship.

The old *kyakuden* had been destroyed in the fire of June 17, 1945, in which Nikkyo, sixty-second-generation high priest of the temple, was burned to death. Although it was rebuilt in 1948, Toda had willed that Soka Gakkai should dedicate a new building made with materials from all countries of the world, to symbolize the goal of world-wide *kosen rufu*.

To finance the construction of the Grand Reception Hall, Soka Gakkai's 1,420,000 member families, during the four

[2] The hypersensitivity of Soka Gakkai to a bad press resulted in a relatively "silent" press as far as coverage of the organization was concerned. For all the newsworthy developments and programs of Soka Gakkai, there was little reported about it in the nation's mass media. In June 1963, the author wrote: "In the past, when a newspaper carried a story which Soka Gakkai found to be inaccurate or misleading, the editor often received a telephone call of strongly worded complaint. Such a reaction on the part of the organization tended to discourage the press from reporting on it. A reporter observed: 'We'd rather not write anything about it to avoid unpleasantness.' . . . Soka Gakkai, under its present leadership, has taken a forward-looking attitude toward press and public relations. . . . Soka Gakkai will cease to be as sensitive to the press as it used to be. . . ." (Kiyoaki Murata: "Soka Gakkai and the Press," *Japan Times,* June 11, 1964.)

days from July 21 to 24, 1961, contributed ￥3,198,824,377 (roughly $9,000,000), which Soka Gakkai claimed was the largest sum ever raised by any religion in the history of Japan.

In the meantime, President Ikeda toured the world in 1960 and 1961 to purchase building materials from thirty-nine nations and to collect stones from these countries to be buried in the foundations of the building.

The five-story building, with a total floor space of 9,808 square meters and a main hall that can accommodate 5,000 persons on the *tatami*-covered floor, cost ￥1,260,756,669 (roughly $3,500,000), and took only one year and ten months to build. The imported building materials include Canadian cedar, Taiwanese cypress, Italian marble, Swedish granite, and Czechoslovakian chandeliers. A fountain Ikeda bought in Rome adorns the front approach to the building.

A dedication ceremony was held on April 2, 1964, to commemorate the "seventh" death anniversary (by the traditional Buddhist method of counting years) of Josei Toda, who had died six years earlier.

Although Ikeda is a devoted heir to his late mentor Toda, his essentially different temperament is having far-reaching effects on the activities of the organization. Whereas Toda impressed many as a religious zealot, Ikeda appears to be a scholarly gentleman and above all strikes those who come to know him with his evident "sincerity." Toda's speeches were characterized by down-to-earth, lively expressions and were usually impromptu. His sentence structure was therefore often irregular and the level of politeness inconsistent.

Ikeda, on the other hand, delivers serious, well-prepared, and well-organized addresses often lasting more than an hour at important meetings. He does interpolate occasional touches of humor, but the level of politeness is consistent throughout.

If this image of Ikeda represents a change in his outward manner since the 1950's, when he was the fearless leader of the vigorous Youth Division, it must still reflect the unchanging inner qualities of humility, sincerity, and prudence.

When he assumed the presidency, Ikeda vowed to lead his

organization as his predecessor had done. Yet in recent years he has carried out bold modifications of the policies and goals set by Toda. His most conspicuous modifications concern 1) attainment of *kosen rufu* by *shakubuku*, 2) the construction of the *hommon no kaidan*, and 3) political activities.

These policy changes are responsible for Soka Gakkai's decidedly new public image and for ending its unpopularity with the mass media. Leaders of Soka Gakkai, however, steadfastly claim that there has been "no change" since the days of Toda in the policy and approach of Soka Gakkai, at least in spirit if not in procedure.

As for *shakubuku*, Ikeda continued to stress its importance. In less than three years, membership rose to 3,000,000 families, the goal set by Ikeda in May 1960 for 1967. As of the end of 1965, 5,500,000 families were members. On May 3, 1966, at the twenty-ninth general meeting of Soka Gakkai, Ikeda announced a new goal—conversion of 10,000,000 families by the end of the year 1979.

This particular year is significant as the seven-hundredth anniversary of 1279, the year in which Nichiren inscribed the Daigohonzon, which, it is said, he bestowed upon mankind. Beyond 1979, Ikeda set another goal: 15,000,000 to be converted by the end of 1990. Despite the immensity of such figures, the rate of conversion required to realize them within the time limit set by Ikeda is considerably slower than that of the period 1955–65, when membership more than tripled.

Under Ikeda's direction, a new tone has begun to mark Soka Gakkai's conversion activities. Of late, he has been cautioning his followers against doing anything unreasonable. This new policy was clearly enunciated in Ikeda's address at the twenty-ninth general meeting of Soka Gakkai headquarters on May 3, 1966, in which he said:

> As a pupil of [Nichiren] Daishonin, I am resolved to build a new Japanese society and develop a new, happy Japan. Therefore it is my wish that all of you who are fighting for the cause of true Buddhism will fully enjoy happiness—not one of you having trouble—and forge ahead.
>
> Let's not have a single victim. Let's not allow even a single member to become a victim. I wish everyone to continue to

keep faith to become happy, as Nichiren Daishonin willed, and engage in Soka Gakkai activities.

At the same time, Ikeda stressed the need for moderation in the conversion drive—a seeming reversal of past policy. He prefaced his remarks by saying: "Our struggle from now on will be a prolonged struggle." In short, he meant: "Let's not rush things."

"We already have more than 5,600,000 families now. So it's no problem to reach the goal [of 10,000,000 by the end of 1979]. . . . There is no need to strain ourselves excessively." Nor was Ikeda afraid to revise membership figures by half a million or so. He said, "I wish to subtract from 300,000 to 500,000 from the gross number of families to arrive at a net figure of five million."

Ikeda meant that a previously announced total membership of 5,600,000 families was not realistic because it included many converts who had either renounced their faith or were no longer active. There were many who somehow lost contact with the organization because of changes of address and for other reasons. The 1966 convention therefore was a turning point in the history of Soka Gakkai. It marked the end of the feverish era of "shakubuku right or wrong." Echoing Ikeda's new policy, the daily organ Seikyo Shimbun, on June 1, 1966, declared in an editorial entitled "Let's Take a Great Forward Step Toward Shakubuku!": "Shakubuku is the spirit of Soka Gakkai. It is the command of [Nichiren] Daishonin. It is the primary force of our kosen rufu. There is no Soka Gakkai without it, much less the happiness of the individual."

Yet the editorial cautioned its readers to conduct shakubuku calmly without rushing themselves. It urged every member of Soka Gakkai to conduct himself properly. "We must realize that an admirable attitude [on our part] itself is the basis for silent and yet splendid shakubuku." In other words, a Soka Gakkai member should seek to convert others by his exemplary behavior rather than by urging others to join Soka Gakkai in so many words.

Since May 1966, Ikeda has on many occasions told his followers to avoid "creating incidents," meaning the kind of affairs that made unfavorable headlines in the past. At a meeting for leaders in 1966, for instance, he said: "Smile, be cheerful, and be moderate in manner. Never utter rude words in giving guidance to and converting others."

The editorial of *Seikyo Shimbun* on January 4, 1967, dealt with the subject of "Shakubuku Activities for This Year" and urged its readers: "Let us carry out *shakubuku* without being bound by narrow viewpoints but always with a broad, flexible attitude." It concluded: "People in their hearts are seeking the right Buddhism. With this conviction, let us endeavor to carry out *shakubuku* this year without forcing ourselves and at a leisurely pace."

The same policy was advocated more recently in the *Seikyo Shimbun* editorial of February 19, 1968, entitled "Let's Conduct Heart-to-Heart Shakubuku":

> It is necessary to understand, when you try to *shakubuku* someone, that *shakubuku* takes place at the instant when the life of the person performing *shakubuku* and that of the person being *shakubuku*-ed come into direct contact with each other. As everyone feels when a man decides to join our faith, there is a heart-warming interflow of trust and mutual understanding between the two.
>
> When a newcomer comes to a discussion meeting [where *shakubuku* is usually conducted], meet the person in a natural manner, and courteously, and speak to him with sincerity. . . . Never be rude in speech or manner; never resort to conduct that is not reasonable. . . .

In an interview with the author on March 27, 1968, Ikeda confirmed this policy, saying that his primary concern was that Soka Gakkai members should conduct themselves as exemplary citizens, whatever the circumstances. This is a radical departure from the stormy years of Toda's presidency.

"One-Third of the Population"

Even more significant is Ikeda's modification of the basic goal of Soka Gakkai—*kosen rufu*, which was understood to mean conversion of the entire Japanese nation and eventually of the whole world, to be symbolized by the erection of the *hommon no kaidan* at the foot of Mount Fuji. Nichiren Shoshu literature quotes Nichiren as saying that his teaching, based on the Lotus Sutra, was to spread throughout East Asia, namely Japan, China, and India. Soka Gakkai reinterpreted this to mean the entire world.

Were the goal of *kosen rufu* applied only to the Japanese nation, the new target Ikeda announced in July 1965 was still extremely significant. Addressing leaders of the Youth Division at Soka Gakkai headquarters in Tokyo, Ikeda introduced the theory of *Shae no san-oku*—literally, "the 300,000 of Shra-vasti."

The phrase is found in *Daichidoron,* a Chinese translation by Kumarajiva of an exegesis by Nagarjuna (about A.D. 150–250) of Mahayana sutras. According to this work, the his-torical Buddha lived and preached for twenty-five years in the ancient Indian kingdom of Shravasti, thought to have been in today's Uttar Pradesh.[3] The population of this state was 900,000, and yet as many as one-third of it had never heard or even seen the Buddha. Thus the "300,000" in the phrase *Shae no san-oku* refers to this one-third of the popula-tion, and the reference is to the difficulty of spreading the teachings of the Buddha—typified by Shravasti, where the Buddha himself lived for so long.

But Ikeda interpreted this pessimistic expression in a positive way. He told his audience:

> The membership of our association now far exceeds five million families [as of July 1965]. There is a formula called *Shae no san-oku* concerning the country of Shae, which was known in the Buddha's lifetime as the country most closely related to him in all of India. That is to say, in the Shae of those years, one-third of its people saw and heard the Buddha and believed in him. Another one-third saw the Buddha but did not hear him preach. The remaining one-third, it is said, neither saw nor heard the Buddha.
>
> If we are to apply this formula to our program of *kosen rufu* and of realizing *obutsu myogo*, it would mean as follows: if one-third of the population of Japan became members of Soka

[3] The name Shae (also read as Shaei) is the Japanese rendering of the Chinese transcription of Shravasti, which was the name of both the capi-tal and the state. Because Buddhism fast disappeared from the area after the Buddha's death, the exact location of Shravasti was not certain. In the mid-nineteenth century, Sir Alexander Cunningham (1814–93) unearthed Buddhist relics near Gonda which identified it as the former site of Shravasti.

Gakkai and another third, though not gaining our faith, supported Komeito, and the remaining third opposed espousing our faith, it would mean virtual *kosen rufu*. We can realize *obutsu myogo* by attaining a *Shae no san-oku* [in Japan]. . . .

Another momentous modification of the goal of Soka Gakkai concerns the all-important issue of the *hommon no kaidan*, which, according to Nichiren Shoshu theology, was to be erected at the foot of Mount Fuji upon completion of *kosen rufu*. In the early years, Toda's and other Soka Gakkai leaders' references to this *kaidan* as *kokuritsu no kaidan*—meaning "state-built" or "national" hall of worship—provoked a great deal of criticism. As a result, Soka Gakkai under Ikeda has dropped the adjective *kokuritsu no* and instead uses the term *hommon no kaidan* (literally, the *kaidan* of the true teaching). In his address at the twenty-ninth general meeting of Soka Gakkai headquarters held on May 3, 1966, Ikeda explained the change of term, saying: "There is not a single mention of *kokuritsu no kaidan* in the writings of [Nichiren] Daishonin. [What Soka Gakkai aims to build] must be a *hommon no kaidan*, to be built by the power of the people. . . ."

The policy change is reflected in one of the standard books on Soka Gakkai published by an affiliated group with the endorsement and blessing of the association itself. The publication is the latest edition of *Nichiren Shoshu Soka Gakkai* by the Tokyo Daigaku Hoke-kyo Kenkyukai (Tokyo University Lotus Sutra Study Society). Its first edition, published in 1962, quotes the key passage in the *Sandai Hihosho*, in which Nichiren stipulates three conditions for the erection of the *hommon no kaidan*. The publication says that two of the three conditions have been fulfilled and the remaining one is *obutsu myogo*. When this is realized, "the *kaidan* would naturally be built with an imperial decree and a Diet resolution."[4]

The revised edition of the same publication, published in 1967, was drastically rewritten. Its section on the *hommon no kaidan* is entitled "Popularly Built Hommon no Kaidan" and contains the following elaboration:

---

[4] Tokyo Daigaku Hoke-kyo Kenkyukaii: *Nichiren Shoshu Soka Gakkai*, Sankibo Busshorin, Tokyo, 1962, pp. 474–75.

Former President Toda, in his thesis *Obutsu Myogo Ron,* said the purpose of our organization was to build the *kokuritsu no kaidan.* Some critics tied this in with Soka Gakkai's entering into politics and advanced the fraudulent argument that [Soka Gakkai] might be planning to make Nichiren Shoshu the state religion. This criticism is evidently wide of the mark. The *kaidan* in the era when the Buddha's teaching prevailed was an ordination platform for priests. And such a platform was contributed by the monarch of a particular state. In the ages of autocracy and feudalism, monarchs represented believers and [all other] people, and the monarch was therefore the donor of the *kaidan.* . . .

The *hommon no kaidan* to be erected in the age of *mappo,* however . . . is clearly one to be erected in the interest of the happiness of the popular masses of the entire world. Therefore the donor would be the people, as would be appropriate in the age of democracy. The word *kokuritsu* [state-built] referred to in [Toda's] *Obutsu Myogo Ron* means "erection by the total will of the people" or "popularly erected." Former President Toda himself declared that without the establishment of the pure faith in the people the erection of a *kaidan* with the power of the state would defeat the purpose and actually destroy the Buddhist teachings.[5]

The New Meaning of "Kaidan"

The best rebuttal, however, of the charge that Soka Gakkai planned to make its own sect the state religion and to establish a national temple by an act of parliament is a plan announced by Ikeda himself in 1964. At the general meeting of May 3, 1964, he revealed the plan to build and dedicate to Taiseki-ji a structure to be called the Shohondo (Grand Main Temple) with funds raised by Soka Gakkai members, in the same way that the proceeds of earlier fund-raising drives had built the Grand Lecture Hall of 1958 and the Grand Reception Hall of 1964. Ikeda announced a four-day fund-raising drive from October 9 to 12, 1965, to raise approximately ¥3,000,000,000 ($8,311,111) for a hall of worship to accommodate five thousand worshipers. He suggested that each member-family save

[5] *Ibid.* (revised edition, 1967), p. 352.

¥700 during the next fourteen months—a monthly saving of about ¥50.

A building committee was formed, and at its first meeting in February 1965 Nittatsu, the high priest of Taiseki-ji, declared that the Shohondo should be considered the *hommon no kaidan* Nichiren had hoped to build. It was agreed to regard it as such. Ikeda has since on several occasions referred to the projected hall as the "virtual *(jijitsujo no) hommon no kaidan.*" For instance, at the thirtieth general meeting of Soka Gakkai headquarters on May 3, 1967, he said: "The Shohondo will be the virtual *hommon no kaidan* and the hall of practice for praying for world peace." Quoting Nichiren's description of the *kaidan* in *Sandai Hihosho* as "the ordination platform where people of the three countries and *ichien budai* repent their sin and have it mitigated," Ikeda explained that the "three countries" were Japan, China, and India and that *ichien budai* meant "the entire world." He went on:

> That is, [Nichiren] said that this *hommon no kaidan* should be a place where people of not only Japan, China, and India but also of the entire world were to repent their sin and have it mitigated. This [*Sandai Hihosho*] makes it clear that the hall is where leaders of the world pray for eternal world peace. Nichiren Daishonin left the task of building this *kaidan* to his followers after his death, saying that one must wait for the time for the erection of the *kaidan*.
>
> For seven hundred years after that, there was no sign that the "time" would come, and it appeared as though Nichiren Daishonin's august will might go unfulfilled. As it is prophesied that "the Buddha's words are never empty," however, myriads of bodhisattvas did arise out of the earth[6] to strive for spreading the great Buddhist law. The Shohondo to be built will be the crystallization of their sincerity and ardor. As a result, we have come to a point where we will complete the seven-hundred-year-old project of building the *kaidan*.
>
> How pleased Nichiren Daishonin must be with this project! How much the Buddha of *sanze-jippo*[7] will praise and admire it! All the guardian deities of the Lotus Sutra will be elated and beat their drums and perform dances of joy.

6 By the bodhisattvas who arose out of the earth, whose advent is prophesied in the Lotus Sutra, Ikeda meant the members of Soka Gakkai.
7 *Sanze-jippo* means literally "three incarnations and ten directions" or "the past, present, and future and the entire universe."

The majestic temples of Thebes in Egypt, the Parthenon of Greece, the great structures of Rome and of Angkor Vat in Cambodia have, with the lapse of time, declined and today are in ruins. The Shohondo, the new hall of practice for world peace, I am convinced, will increase its brilliance as time passes and will continue to be an immortal edifice to eternity beyond the ten thousand years of the era of *mappo*.

I don't know how much attention people of today's Japan and the world will pay to this magnificent task of ours. But the erection of the Shohondo, the *hommon no kaidan*, will be the construction of the pillars of Japan and will signify the rising of the sun to illumine the dark world. I am convinced that the historians and people of the future will testify to the admiration, blissfulness, and joy represented by the building.

As the fund-raising drive approached, Soka Gakkai leaders, through publications and at meetings, impressed upon members the importance of contributing to the fund. For instance, a *Seikyo Shimbun* editorial of October 1, 1965, intoned:

There is no greater elation and honor for a believer in the Buddhism established by Nichiren Shonin than to be able to participate in this offertory. This is the ultimate summation of the seven-hundred-year history of Nichiren Shoshu. . . . This great fortune of ours to be born in this particular time cannot be bought by any amount of material assets. . . . The offertory to the Shohondo is the greatest undertaking allowed us in our lifetime. This is the best opportunity for us to express our gratitude for the benefit bestowed [by Nichiren]. We must not think in terms of immediate benefits, but we must give to the limit of our capacity by being convinced that this will bring eternal great fortune to our posterity for the endless future.

At Ikeda's suggestion, for some months before the four-day collection period the Mitsubishi Bank, which was to handle the cash, distributed among Soka Gakkai members specially made piggy banks to facilitate their monthly savings.

The collection, held as scheduled at more than sixteen thousand places throughout the country, brought in a total of ¥35,064,305,882 from Soka Gakkai members. The association of Nichiren Shoshu priests also contributed ¥157,878,265, and the Hokke-ko, the pre-Soka Gakkai associations of lay adherents of Nichiren Shoshu, collected ¥313,820,162. The grand total was ¥35,536,004,309 (approximately $100,000,000) or more than ten times the target sum. The total number of contributors was given as approximately 8,000,000.

Many incredulous observers, while admitting that Soka Gakkai was one of the largest religious organizations in Japan, found it difficult to swallow the sum of more than ¥35,000,000,000. It was rumored at that time that the total included nine-digit contributions by wealthy members. Soka Gakkai said there were a number of such large sums but revealed no details on the ground that what is important is not the amount of a contribution but how much of what one has at his disposal one gives.

In the meantime, the building committee went ahead with designing the structure and computing the cost of construction, as well as buying land to expand the Taiseki-ji grounds.

On October 12, 1967, the invocation ceremony for the building of the Shohondo was held at Taiseki-ji, attended by 6,600 leading members of Soka Gakkai (in honor of the sixty-sixth-generation high priest of Taiseki-ji), with members from overseas chapters bringing the total to 8,888.

The construction project, under contract to six leading building companies (on a joint-venture basis), is scheduled for completion in 1972. The basic plan for the sanctuary, announced on February 16, 1967. showed the building designed by Kimio Yokoyama (also designer of the Grand Reception Hall) as approximately one hundred meters square and, at its highest point, sixty-six meters high—again in honor of Taiseki-ji's sixty-sixth-generation high priest.

The main sanctuary, beneath a suspended roof, will accommodate six thousand persons, all with an unobstructed view of the platform on which the Daigohonzon will be placed. The entrance hall will also accommodate six thousand worshipers awaiting their turn to enter the inner sanctum.

By October 12, 1967, Soka Gakkai had collected pebbles and stones from 135 countries and regions of the world through the efforts of its members, including a piece of rock from Antarctica. These are to be buried in the foundations of the temple to symbolize the goal of world-wide propagation of Nichiren Shoshu. The names of the more than eight million persons who contributed to the Shohondo building fund, entered in 133 solidly bound volumes, will also be kept in the Shohondo "for eternity."

Thus Soka Gakkai and the administrative authorities of Nichiren Shoshu plan to build the Shohondo, which will be the *hommon no kaidan,* with private funds by the end of 1972. This seems to clear Soka Gakkai of the charge that it plans to build a national hall of worship through an act of parliament.

But how can the construction now of the "ultimate" hall of worship be reconciled with the doctrine of Nichiren Shoshu, which says that the *hommon no kaidan* is to be erected when *kosen rufu* is accomplished? Ikeda, on the other hand, had introduced the theory of *Shae no san-oku*—that is, the goal of conversion of one-third of the population. Does this mean then that Soka Gakkai hopes to attain the one-third objective by the time the Shohondo is completed?

When presented with this question, Ikeda appeared to see no problem. "We build the Shohondo first and then get people to come to worship in it. We get the container first and the contents later, as it were. It does not matter if the completion of the *hommon no kaidan* and conversion of one-third of the population do not coincide."

DIFFERENCES FROM TODA

Some of the temperamental differences between the two successive leaders of Soka Gakkai, Toda and Ikeda, have already been pointed out. But there are still others. Ikeda appears to be a more humble man than Toda, who tended to bully his followers at meetings, shouting: "When the time comes, are you going to stand up to it? Are you?" By contrast, Ikeda addresses his followers with deference, as at Soka Gakkai's general meeting on May 3, 1966: "Although I am powerless and ignorant, I will carry on earnestly. . . . I humbly ask you to support me. . . . *Kosen rufu* is the Buddha's will. It cannot be achieved by the power of a common man like me."

Whereas Toda treated the Nichiren Shoshu priesthood with some contempt, Ikeda displays a very reverent attitude toward the church. He has repeatedly referred to his "duty" and that of his association to "safeguard" the temple and its high priest. At the same general meeting of 1966, Ikeda told the audience:

> We are not a sect. We are an association of lay members of a sect. Our duty is to safeguard the temple, the high priest. I will bear the brunt of all the abuses and insults [that might be directed against the high priest]. If I don't, the priests [of Nichiren Shoshu], who number only a few hundred, cannot protect this large number of lay adherents and fight against the *sansho shima* [three obstacles and four devils]. In the worst event, the sect might be cast to the winds. Let us keep on safeguarding them!

Again, whereas Toda was a religious zealot, Ikeda, despite his obvious devotion to his faith, is the soul of common sense. He told a meeting of headquarters leaders on June 30, 1967:

> Even though you espouse our faith, if you become rigid and inflexible in your manner, there is the danger of your becoming isolated from society. What we advocate is something everyone can agree on. We must always bear in mind that we are living in society.

Then he cautioned Soka Gakkai leaders against overzealousness:

> I don't want you to stay up late at night. There is the rule that all our functions and programs must end before 9:30 p.m. Headquarters will not be responsible for what may happen after that.
>
> Accidents usually occur when you do not abide by our guidance and when you are out late at night. I am always concerned about your safety. I want members of the Women's Division and Young Women's Division in particular to go home early. When a meeting ends at 9:30 p.m., feel free to go right home. If you are fatigued and doze off at the wheel and cause a traffic accident, you suffer. Buddhism holds life precious. If you sit up late at night and do not take good care of your life and health, that is breaking Buddhist law. If a leader violates that basic principle, how can others—common members—understand the teachings of [Nichiren] Daishonin?

Even on the supreme goal of *kosen rufu*, Ikeda displays moderation. Addressing headquarters leaders on July 26, 1965, he said that it was indeed his earnest wish to report to the high

priest of Taiseki-ji that *"kosen rufu* has now been achieved."
"Yet," he stressed, "I cannot say when this may take place.
But I think it is right to move on with the goal I have just
described before us. And I wish you to hand down to your
children and grandchildren the same spirit—that *kosen rufu*
will surely be achieved some day."

The Organization
of Soka Gakkai

MEMBERSHIP

From its modest beginnings in the early years of postwar reconstruction when Toda had only a handful of followers, Soka Gakkai mushroomed into a huge organization claiming a membership of 6,876,000 families in January 1969.

Soka Gakkai has always announced its membership in terms of *shotai* (families or households), often baffling the observers who attempt to figure out its membership in terms of individuals. This, however, is the traditional Japanese system of indicating the size of a religious organization and reflects the social structure of Japan, in which the family, not the individual, has been the basic element. The size of a Shinto or Buddhist parish, for instance, is always expressed by the number of families it includes.

Officers of Soka Gakkai have never announced the number of individual members and comment that when an individual—a married man, for instance—joins Soka Gakkai, it is generally expected that eventually his wife too will join his faith. When adult members of a family join the association, their offspring may very well be expected to follow suit. On the other hand, when a young man or woman, living apart from his or her parents, joins Soka Gakkai, it is not assumed that the parents will also join as a result.

Statistics compiled by the Religions Section of the Cultural Affairs Bureau of the Ministry of Education list the number of adherents of Nichiren Shoshu at the end of 1966 as 15,234,136, a figure obtained by multiplying the reported number of families by an index of 3.94, the average size of Japanese families derived from quadrennial surveys by the Statistics Bureau of the Prime Minister's Office. This number of families professing Nichiren Shoshu—3,860,000—however, is considerably smaller than the figure of 6,000,000 released by Soka Gakkai at the end of 1966. What is more, the Ministry of Education figure includes non-Soka Gakkai adherents of Nichiren Shoshu.[1]

If one used an arbitrary index of 2.5 persons per Soka Gakkai family, however, the total individual membership for 6,876,000 families would be 17,190,000—about seventeen percent of the total population. If the number of members is calculated by this method, then the present membership must be roughly doubled in order for Soka Gakkai to attain the "one-third-of-the-nation" goal.

It must also be borne in mind that the membership figure given at any particular time represents the number of *honzon* given to converts by Nichiren Shoshu temples throughout the country when they are admitted into the faith. This figure includes individuals who have renounced their faith or ceased to be active members of Soka Gakkai, those who have died, and those who have lost contact with the association.

For this reason, Ikeda announced on May 3, 1966, the policy of subtracting from the aggregate membership figure as many as half a million to arrive at a more realistic assessment of the strength of his organization. Soka Gakkai does, however, announce the membership figures of the component divisions and departments, such as the Student Division, Women's Division, and Youth Division, in terms of individuals. The membership of the Student Division, for instance, was announced as 230,000 on September 8, 1968. Youth Division membership, comprising the Young Men's and Young Women's divisions, was said to be 3,900,000 (2,400,000 men and 1,500,000 women) as of September 8, 1968.

Some indication of the total number of individual members, however, has been given. On July 3, 1966, for instance, Ikeda

[1] Ministry of Education: *Shukyo Nenkan, 1966* (Almanac of Religions, 1966), p. 105.

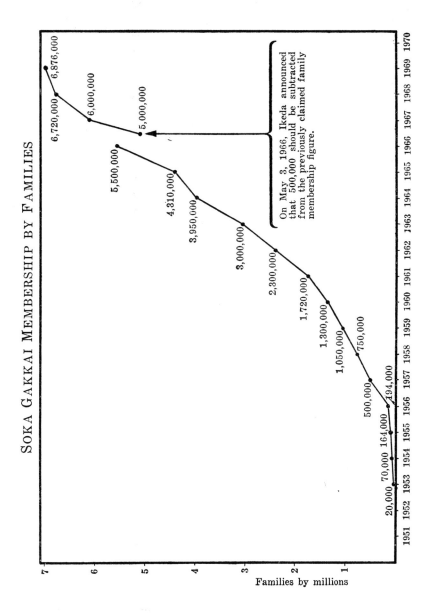

SOKA GAKKAI MEMBERSHIP BY FAMILIES

Families by millions

On May 3, 1966, Ikeda announced that 500,000 should be subtracted from the previously claimed family membership figure.

referred to "eight million bodhisattvas out of the earth . . . now joyfully and valiantly engaged in the battle for spreading the true Buddhism." The statement implies that there are about eight million active Soka Gakkai members. This figure was probably based on the number of persons who participated in the October 1965 fund-raising campaign for the Shohondo.

Ikeda also spoke of "eight million bodhisattvas out of the earth" in the preface to his *Rissho Ankoku Ron Kogi* (Lectures on the *Rissho Ankoku Ron*), referring to members of Soka Gakkai or adherents of Nichiren Shoshu. But in the same volume he also mentions "ten million members of Soka Gakkai."[2] In his address at the May 3, 1968, general meeting of Soka Gakkai, Ikeda mentioned "ten million members," as did another speaker on the same program.

STRUCTURE

The structure of Soka Gakkai is based on the "vertical line" and the "horizontal line." The vertical line, which will be discussed first here, means all the individuals who are linked by successive instances of *shakubuku*. Such a line begins when A converts B, who in turn converts C, and so on. This vertical line holds regardless of where the individuals concerned may be located. Soka Gakkai claims that the bond established through *shakubuku* is so strong that "no one can ever sever it." It also says that the bond is stronger than consanguineous kinship because a Soka Gakkai member is a person who has chosen the particular faith even at the expense of renouncing his own family religion.

The vertical line starts from a *kumi* (unit), made up of approximately ten to a dozen families, at the bottom. From five to ten *kumi* make up one *han* (group). The next unit up the line is the *chiku* (district), with from one hundred to two hundred families. Above the *chiku* is the *shibu* (chapter), consisting of approximately one thousand up to two thousand families. A number of chapters form a *soshibu* (general chapter), which is under the *hombu* (headquarters). Several

[2] Daisaku Ikeda: *Rissho Ankoku Ron Kogi* (Lectures on the *Rissho Ankoku Ron*), Soka Gakkai, Tokyo, 1966, p. 72.

hombu form a *sogohombu* (joint headquarters), which is directly controlled by the top leadership of the organization.

The principal activity of Soka Gakkai at the lowest level is the *zadankai* (discussion meeting), attended by members of a unit and a group, where members testify to their religious experiences, discuss problems, and "deepen their faith." They study doctrine, using Soka Gakkai texts and other materials. Nonmembers are often invited and converted to Nichiren Shoshu on the spot. Leaders of the association conduct meetings every Saturday with every district, giving "guidance."

There are shortcomings in this particular organization. Two vertical lines might come into conflict over a potential convert. Again, it does not link together all members residing in one area. Two neighbors may be unaware that each is a member, or, even if they are, each may attend different meetings. To offset this difficulty, in 1955 Soka Gakkai introduced in Tokyo the horizontal-line system, called the *burokku* (block) system.

The block system starts at the lowest level with the minor block, then mounts by block, major block, and general block to joint block, which is subject to supervision by joint headquarters at the apex of the system. Thus each Soka Gakkai member family belongs to both a unit and a minor block, the basic units of the two systems. As a component of the organization, each family has a dual function. It may engage in the activities of a unit or of a minor block.

Furthermore, each member of Soka Gakkai belongs to a division, such as the Men's, Women's, Young Men's, and the like. The Youth Division now consists of the Young Men's Division, Boys' and Girls' Division, Junior High Division, Senior High Division, Student Division, and Young Women's Division.

An adult male member belongs to the Men's Division, a housewife to the Women's Division, a high school student to the Junior High or the Senior High Division, and so on. Some divisions are organized on military lines, using terms such as *buntai* (squad), *han* (team),[3] *tai* (company), *butai* (corps), *bu* (subdivision), and *hombu* (headquarters).

As of August 1968, Soka Gakkai had a total of 3,984

[3] Soka Gakkai's official English names for *buntai* and *han* are "unit" and "group," respectively.

chapters, of which 229 were located outside Japan. There are many other departments to deal with Soka Gakkai's various functions. Probably the most important is the Study Department,[4] made up of members who have attained various ranks through progressive examinations in doctrinal understanding and knowledge.

The result of the first appointment examination, held in December 1952, increased the initial Study Department membership of 24 to 65. With each semiannual examination in subsequent years, the department's membership snowballed. By 1961, it was 40,000, and in March 1968 the figure stood at 1,447,000, with 6,400 members overseas.

Soka Gakkai's emphasis on the study of doctrine has two aims. First, such study gives a solid grounding to the faith of each member and confirms his identification with the organization and its moral strength. Second, the academic ranking system imparts to many members a self-confidence which their non-Soka Gakkai activities may not provide. A grocer with only a primary-school education may become a "professor" if he passes the required examination on Nichiren Shoshu theology. The satisfaction such a member derives from giving doctrinal guidance to a new convert—for example, a university student who has yet to pass the first examination of the Study Department—is easy to imagine.

FINANCES

Soka Gakkai is one of the most affluent associations in Japan, although its members do not pay dues as such. Its annual budget is said to be about ￥2,600,000,000 ($7,222,000), but real income is perhaps considerably higher. Of this amount, about ￥1,600,000,000 is contributed by the Finance Department, whose approximately 400,000 individual members are replaced annually. Each member of this department is required to pay ￥4,000 (slightly over $11) annually in four installments. A further ￥1,000,000,000 is believed to come from the sale of Soka Gakkai books and periodicals.

---

[4] For the circumstances under which the Study Department was established, see page 101.

The principal publication is the daily *Seikyo Shimbun,* claiming a circulation of 3,580,000 in September 1968. This figure does not necessarily reflect the number of individual members who buy the paper. Some buy extra copies to distribute among nonmembers in an effort to convert them.

Another important publication is the pictorial weekly *Seikyo Gurafu* (The Seiko Graphic), with a circulation of 1,080,000. There is also the theoretical monthly *Daibyakurenge* (Great White Lotus Blossom), with a circulation of 2,000,000. Soka Gakkai has other publications, either weekly or monthly, intended for nonmembers. These include the monthly *Ushio* (Tide), now considered a respectable "intellectual" magazine, and a magazine for primary-school children, *Kibo no Tomo* (Friend of Hope), which claims a circulation of 400,000.

Also important is the revenue from the publication of many books on doctrinal texts and their exegeses by Makiguchi, Toda, Ikeda, and others. The collected writings of Nichiren, the basic scripture for today's Soka Gakkai—published in Toda's era—is a must for any serious-minded member at ¥2,000 ($5.55) a copy. Speeches by leaders, including Ikeda, are liberally sprinkled with quotations from this volume, and the verbatim reports of the speeches in *Seikyo Shimbun* give the page reference for each quotation.

The first four volumes of Ikeda's *Ningen Kakumei,* a history of Soka Gakkai in fictional form, published between 1965 and 1968, sold over a million copies each. Ikeda contributed all the royalties to the association's treasury.

Of the ¥2,600,000,000 annual income, about ¥2,000,000,000 is spent on real estate and buildings, including new Nichiren Shoshu temples. On May 3, 1968, Ikeda announced that the total number of Nichiren Shoshu temples—a mere 75 in 1942—had increased to 319, mainly through Soka Gakkai's temple-building efforts. Soka Gakkai's affluence is also reflected in Ikeda's announcement on May 3, 1968, that the land owned by Taiseki-ji had increased from 120,000 *tsubo* (approximately 98 acres) in 1960 to 640,000 *tsubo* (about 522 acres) in 1965 and to 1,066,682 *tsubo* (about 870 acres) in May 1968. This increased acreage includes the land on which the Shohondo is to be built.

Soka Gakkai spends much of its revenue on its educational

program, including the building of the lower and upper secondary schools (rough equivalents of junior and senior high schools) which opened in April 1968 and the building of Soka University, which is to open in 1971. On May 3, 1966, Ikeda told a general meeting:

> We will not seek one *sen* [one-hundredth of one yen] of contribution from you to build the university. We are trying hard to save money with the publication of books and newspapers. We receive dues from members of the Finance Department, but these merely cover the costs of holding chapter meetings and normai operational costs. For all the special projects, publication is the source of revenue. But please have no worry.

CULTURAL AND PUBLICATION ACTIVITIES

Soka Gakkai has several affiliated organizations besides the political party Komeito. One of these is the Seikyo Shimbun-sha (Seikyo Press), which handles most of the association's publishing activities, including the editing of its daily and monthly organs as well as numerous books on doctrine and writings of the leaders. Seikyo Shimbun-sha's English-language publications include the *Seikyo Times*, a monthly; the *World Tribune*, a three-times-a-week periodical published in Los Angeles; and such books by Daisaku Ikeda as *Lectures on Buddhism* (four volumes), *The Human Revolution* (four volumes), *Science and Religion,* and the *Complete Works of Daisaku Ikeda.* Makiguchi's *Kachiron,* referred to in Chapter 5, has also been published in an English version as *The Philosophy of Value.* Ikeda's *Ningen Kakumei* (The Human Revolution) has been published in French as *La Révolution Humaine* (three volumes).

Soka Gakkai's periodicals in other languages include *L'Avenir* (monthly) in French, published in Paris; *Seikyo Zeitung* (monthly) in German, published in Düsseldorf; *Li Min Sheng Pao* (monthly) in Chinese, published in Hong Kong; *Brasil Seikyo* (weekly) in Portuguese, published in São Paulo; *Peru Seikyo* (bimonthly) in Spanish, published in Lima; and *Argentina Seikyo* (bimonthly) in Spanish, published in Buenos Aires. The Seikyo Shimbun-sha has also published introductory booklets about Soka Gakkai in English, French, German, Chinese, Portuguese, Spanish, and Indonesian.

The arts are another sphere of Soka Gakkai's nonreligious activities. Its affiliate, the Min'on Concert Association, inaugurated on September 1, 1963, has been giving a growing number and variety of musical programs on a membership basis. In October 1968, it had 1,800,000 members and was giving from 15 to 25 performances a month in Tokyo, more than 250 performances throughout the country, and more than 3,000 in one year. Another cultural affiliate is the Min'en Theatrical Association, founded on June 27, 1964. Like Min'on, it presents theatrical programs on a membership basis. Both organizations offer the masses the opportunity to hear good music and see good dramatic productions and ballets at relatively little cost.

Besides producing concerts with Japanese artists, the Min'on Concert Association also invites such foreign companies as the Novosibirsk Ballet Theater of the Soviet Union (1966), the Twentieth-Century Ballet of Belgium (1967), and the American Ballet Theater (1968). None of these programs give any indication that they are sponsored by Soka Gakkai.

The same may be said of the monthly magazine *Ushio*. It began in 1960 as an eighteen-page theoretical magazine on politics published for members of Soka Gakkai and carried articles by leaders of the organization. After January 1963, however, it was transformed from a sectarian publication into a typical Japanese intellectual magazine. Few Soka Gakkai leaders contribute articles. Japanese intellectuals, although at first reluctant, now write for the magazine, and the contents give no hint that the monthly is a Soka Gakkai publication. Its publisher is given as Ushio Shuppan-sha.

THE LIFE OF A MEMBER

A potential Soka Gakkai convert is usually taken to a discussion meeting by the member attempting to *shakubuku* him. At the meeting he listens to the testimony given by members, has his own doubts and questions resolved, and probably decides to join the association. The member who brought him is his "introducer," and becomes the convert's immediate superior in their *kumi* (unit).

Before he can be admitted to Nichiren Shoshu, a new convert must remove all the images, tablets, and mandalas in his own family Shinto or Buddhist altars. This procedure is called *hobobarai,* "removal of evil religion."[5]

After *hobobarai,* his introducer takes the convert to a nearby Nichiren Shoshu temple where the priest performs the conversion rites and he receives a *gohonzon.* The convert pays ¥500 as offertory to the temple. When he hangs the *gohonzon* in his family altar, he must hold a *shikimi* (anise) twig between his lips so that his breath will not desecrate the sacred object. Nichiren Shoshu tradition does not permit flowers to be offered to the *gohonzon.* The reason given is that flowers wither and their colors fade. The only plant that may be placed before it is the *shikimi,* the evergreen tree used in Buddhist services in Japan. From day to day, the worshiper may offer the *gohonzon* incense sticks, candles, water, and bowls of rice. These are common items, but according to Soka Gakkai anything may be offered as long as it reflects the spirit of offering something to Nichiren.

Soka Gakkai members' chief religious practice is *gongyo:* the recitation of the title of the Lotus Sutra and passages from it in the morning and in the evening.

The morning *gongyo* consists of five prayers. In the first prayer, the votary sits on the floor in front of the *gohonzon* and recites "Nam-myoho Renge-kyo" three times. Then he turns to the east and reads aloud a passage from the second chapter (Hobembon) of the Lotus Sutra and from the sixteenth chapter (Juryobon). This is followed by three *hiki-daimoku* (drawn-out recitations of "Nam-myoho Renge-kyo") in which one pronounces the sacred phrase by giving double value to the length of each syllable: "Na-a-mu-u-myo-o-ho-o Re-en-ge-e-kyo-o." Then comes a silent reading of a prayer.

In the second prayer, the votary turns to face the *gohonzon* again, sounds a table bell once, and reads the Hobembon passage. The reading of the Juryobon passage is preceded by another sounding of the bell. This time he must read the entire

[5] For more about *hobobarai* and the problems it entails, see "Shakubuku: Its Meaning and Method" in Chapter 6.

24. *Daisaku Ikeda, third and current president of Soka Gakkai.*

Toward the Human Revolution

25. *Tsunesaburo Makiguchi, founder and first president of Soka Gakkai.*

26. *Josei Toda, second president of Soka Gakkai.*

27. Tomb of Josei Toda at Taiseki-ji, Shizuoka Prefecture.

28. President Ikeda (right) at a meeting of Soka Gakkai leaders at the organization's Tokyo headquarters.

29. *President Ikeda gives guidance to representatives of Soka Gakkai's Senior High Division, which in 1968 had 160,000 members.*

30. *President Ikeda addresses a meeting of Soka Gakkai members at the Kanagawa Prefecture Joint Headquarters.*

31. President Ikeda participates in the groundbreaking ceremony for the Shohondo (Grand Main Temple) at Taiseki-ji.

32. President Ikeda encourages Soka Gakkai members taking an examination on Nichiren Shoshu doctrine. Here the examination questions are written on a blackboard.

33. Soka Gakkai's Student Division holds a meeting (August 1967) of representatives of its 200,000 members at the auditorium of Nihon University in Tokyo. The division aims to double its membership.

34. *A Soka Gakkai leader conducts a study meeting. The writings in the background present some of the key elements of Nichiren Shoshu doctrine.*

35. *An editorial meeting at the headquarters of the Seikyo Press, the publication center of Soka Gakkai.*

36. *Komeito, Soka Gakkai's political party, establishes contact with voters at one of its public counseling centers, to which citizens can bring their complaints and problems.*

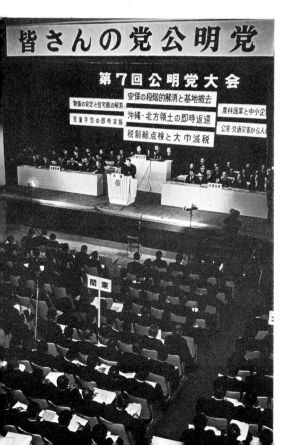

37. *Komeito holds its seventh convention on January 21, 1969, at Toshima Public Hall, Tokyo.*

38. *Successful Komeito candidates congratulate one another at their party headquarters as their victory in the July 1968 House of Councilors election is confirmed.*

39. *Komeito is noted for the alacrity with which its representatives reach a disaster area—usually with relief goods. Here relief goods are being distributed to flood victims. The banner on the truck announces that Komeito is the donor.*

Juryobon chapter of the sutra. Then he recites *hikidaimoku* three times, sounds a bell once, and reads the second prayer. Then he chants the *daimoku* three times. The third, fourth, and fifth prayers are different in contents.

Evening *gongyo* consists of the second, third, and fifth prayers of morning *gongyo*, conducted exactly the same as in the morning. Obviously, under many circumstances, a Soka Gakkai member would find it difficult to conduct the prescribed morning and evening services. A factory worker living in a dormitory or a patient in a hospital ward are just two examples. Even at home, a member whose family objected to his joining Soka Gakkai would find it difficult to fulfill his religious duties. In such cases, Soka Gakkai tells its members that "it is not necessary to recite the *daimoku* loudly or to burn incense sticks or candles. . . . When you conduct *gongyo* despite objections, you may find yourself being kicked out of a dormitory, or discharged by your employer, or other members of your family might touch the *gohonzon*." Such developments could break a member's faith, and he might eventually renounce it. If people complain about a member's loud *daimoku* recitation, then the member should recite softly, Soka Gakkai advises. "What is important, above all, is not to let such circumstances be the cause of your losing your *gohonzon* (meaning ceasing to be a member of the association). If you are resolved never to part with your *gohonzon*, come what may, a way will open itself in front of you, even though you might suffer temporarily."[6]

Another key requirement for a member is to conduct *shakubuku*, just as he himself was *shakubuku*-ed.[7]

Equally important is a pilgrimage to the head temple, Taiseki-ji. The temple is a twenty-minute bus ride from Fujinomiya station on the Minobu line of the Japanese National Railways. Groups of pilgrims come to Taiseki-ji at the rate of fifteen thousand persons a day. All together, up to 3,500,000 devotees visit the temple every year. Those from distant parts of the country stay overnight in the

[6] From a *Seikyo Shimbun* editorial quoted in Kodaira, *op. cit.*, pp. 147–48.

[7] For details about *shakubuku*, see "Shakubuku: Its Meaning and Method" in Chapter 6.

dormitories of the temple. Short-distance visitors have a choice between a day trip and an overnight trip.

Most pilgrims come to Fujinomiya on trains chartered from the Japanese National Railways. Highly efficient teams of members from the Pilgrimage Department conduct the pilgrims from Fujinomiya to the temple. For this group travel on such an unprecedented scale, the government railways built special waiting rooms at key junctions and recently rebuilt tracks at Fuji station on the trunk Tokaido line so that the pilgrims' trains could be switched from the main line to the branch line instead of requiring the passengers to change trains.

In September 1965, for the first time, Soka Gakkai chartered a ship to transport pilgrims from Kochi, in Shikoku, to Taganoura, in Shizuoka Prefecture, the nearest port to Taiseki-ji. During the two years and four months after this, the ship, the *Fuji,* carrying up to 1,300 passengers and traveling at 20.4 knots, made 140 trips between Shikoku and Shizuoka, transporting more than 160,000 pilgrims. Later, the *Fuji's* service was extended to Kagoshima, Miyazaki, and Okinawa. More recently, another ship was added to the same service.

The primary object of the pilgrimage is to worship the Daigohonzon now kept in the sanctuary, a privilege exclusive to members of the sect. However, the visit to Taiseki-ji also stimulates each member's sense of belonging and commitment to a movement that is historical, large, and stable. An impressive gate opens onto the long walk through the temple grounds, flanked by rows of temple buildings and towering cedar trees, centuries old. The pilgrim's exhilaration is complete when he enters the Grand Reception Hall, a colossal piece of masonry combining both ancient tradition and modern styling.

MOTIVES FOR JOINING SOKA GAKKAI

How does someone become a member of Soka Gakkai? What motive does he have? One answer may be found in the "motive survey" conducted by Soka Gakkai in 1967 and reported in the *Seikyo Shimbun* of August 23, 1967.[8] A questionnaire was answered by a sample of one hundred persons chosen at random from the 11,236 members of the Men's Division who had joined Soka Gakkai during May 1967 through the joint headquarters in Tokyo alone. The following six questions were asked:

1. What problem did you have before you joined?
2. On what occasion did you decide to join?
3. How many times had you been told about our faith before you decided to espouse it?[9]
4. What was your introducer [the person who converted you] to you?
5. What was your religion before you joined Soka Gakkai?
6. What degree of interest did you have in your former religion?

To the first question, forty-six percent answered "anxiety about the future," while thirty-four percent gave their major problem as lack of friends. Twenty percent mentioned financial difficulties. Fifteen percent mentioned ill health and another fifteen percent disharmony with the rest of their families. Fourteen percent listed other problems.[10]

Had a similar survey been conducted ten years earlier, the percentages for financial difficulties and ill health would probably have been much higher. The 1967 figures suggest that a change has occurred, in the last decade, in the social strata from which Soka Gakkai draws its members. The poll also reflects the social and economic changes that have taken place in Japan over the same period.

In answer to question 2, a majority of fifty-nine percent said they had joined the organization because they were convinced by the sincerity of those who tried to *shakubuku* them. Fifteen percent said they joined because other members of their families already belonged to Soka Gakkai. Ten percent attributed their conversion to reading the *Seikyo Shimbun* and *Seikyo Gurafu* (the pictorial weekly). Seven percent were won by "the cheerful mood of a discussion meeting" of Soka

[8] This survey sheds little light on the motives of men and women who joined Soka Gakkai in the early 1950's.
[9] That is, how many times were *shakubuku* attempts made on you?
[10] The total of percentages exceeds one hundred presumably because many gave more than one answer.

Gakkai, three percent by "watching the way other Soka Gakkai members worked at their places of employment," and two percent "because of the good job being done by Komeito." Four percent gave other reasons.

To question 3, seventy percent replied that up to five attempts to *shakubuku* them were made. Nineteen percent joined after six to ten attempts to convert them. Eight percent joined only after more than sixteen *shakubuku* attempts had been made. Three percent said they had been subjected to *shakubuku* attempts from eleven to fifteen times.

Answers to question 4 showed that friends were the easiest to *shakubuku*. This group constituted forty-eight percent. Twenty-two percent said they had been *shakubuku*-ed by their fellow workers, eleven percent by family members, six percent by neighbors, five percent by relatives, and the remaining eight percent by "others."

Answers to question 5 showed that ninety percent of the converts had been affiliated with other Buddhist sects and Shinto. Because Buddhism and Shinto have little truly religious hold on their nominal adherents in modern Japan, the statistics mean that a vast majority of Soka Gakkai members had very little interest in religion. This assumption is consistent with the statistics derived with regard to question 6 (What degree of interest did you have in your former religion?). Sixty-eight percent said they had had no interest; nineteen percent replied that they had been "interested a little"; and twelve percent replied that only other members (or one other member) of their families had been interested in any religion. Only one percent—that is, a single individual in the one-hundred-person sample—had been serious about another religion before joining Soka Gakkai.

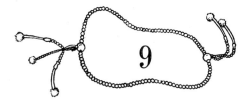

Soka Gakkai and Politics

THE DOCTRINAL BASIS OF POLITICAL INTEREST

In its early years Soka Gakkai was popularly classified as one of Japan's many postwar "new religions" and received scant attention from Japanese intellectuals. Today, however, it commands the awed attention of intellectuals and political parties and of overseas observers as well. Two factors are chiefly responsible for the new climate of opinion regarding Soka Gakkai. One is the transformed behavior of the association itself. The second is the political potential of the religious organization demonstrated by its political arm Komeito, whose official English name is the Clean Government Party.

Soka Gakkai created Komeito on November 17, 1964. As of January 1969, the party had twenty-four seats in the House of Councilors and twenty-five seats in the House of Representatives. In the lower house, Komeito is the third largest opposition party after the Japan Socialist Party and the Japan Democratic Socialist Party. On February 13, 1968, Chairman Yoshikatsu Takeiri of Komeito announced his hope that the party would become the number one opposition party in the Diet within ten years.

The formation of a political party by a religious organization, without precedent in Japan, initially caused much controversy, as it seemed to raise a constitutional question. Article 20 of the constitution stipulates:

> Freedom of religion is guaranteed to all. No religious organization shall receive any privilege from the State nor exercise any political authority.

161

No person shall be compelled to take part in any religious act, celebration, rite, or practice.

The State and its organs shall refrain from religious education or any other religious activity.

Many people claimed that the establishment of Komeito threatened to infringe this constitutional provision and warned that Soka Gakkai aimed to control the state and to impose its own religion, Nichiren Shoshu, on the entire nation. Some argued that a political party representing a religious organization violated this constitutional guarantee of freedom of worship as soon as it gained seats in parliament, because it meant that "a religious organization exercises political authority."

Soka Gakkai leaders replied to such arguments by pointing to Christian political parties in European nations, and by declaring that they had no intention of imposing their own faith on the entire nation even if they obtained a majority in the national legislature. Soka Gakkai, they held, would be the last group to disregard the constitutional guarantee of freedom of worship, because its first leaders had been victims of the religious intolerance of prewar and wartime Japan's nationalistic regime.

The history of Nichirenism suggests that Nichiren devotees are bound to be politically active. Nichiren himself thought it his duty to admonish the government that had failed to espouse his own Buddhist canon, that of the Lotus Sutra. An earnest adherent of Nichiren in any age would feel obliged to do likewise.

This religious intervention in the affairs of the state is called *kokka kangyo* in traditional Japanese vocabulary. Not only did Nichiren himself resort to *kokka kangyo* through his famous treatise called *Rissho Ankoku Ron,* but so did his successors from time to time. Soka Gakkai and Nichiren Shoshu leaders, in criticizing the politics of contemporary Japan, often invoke *Rissho Ankoku Ron* to exhort themselves and their followers to rectify the present government and politics in Japan.

The aim of Soka Gakkai's political activities was clearly stated by its second president, Josei Toda, in his April 8, 1965, address in Osaka. He said the salvation of the masses was the objective every disciple of Nichiren must actively pursue. At the time when Nichiren himself was spreading the teachings of the Lotus Sutra, he determined that the *hommon no kaidan* should be erected. "And now is the time when we must, come what may, achieve that end," Toda told his audience.

"Now," Toda went on, "the method used in former times in achieving *kosen rufu* was to convert the ruler of a country and thereby to attain it at one fell swoop. . . . But today we cannot achieve *kosen rufu* even though His Majesty the Emperor worshiped our *gohonzon*. The reason is that sovereignty has been shifted [from the emperor] to the people. This is the reason why we must consider politics." Toda said he expected members of Soka Gakkai to take part in popular elections "for the sake of *kosen rufu*."

Soka Gakkai's actual participation in popular government began with the elections to local legislatures in April 1955. Soka Gakkai ran fifty-one of its members of the Culture Bureau as candidates for the ward assemblies of Tokyo and for the city councils of cities within metropolitan Tokyo and elsewhere. All were elected.

In the July 10, 1956, House of Councilors election, Soka Gakkai ran six candidates (four from the national constituency and two from the local districts). In this election, three were successful, winning for Soka Gakkai its first toehold in the national legislature. The election results heightened public awareness of the already notorious religious organization, and its obvious political potential aroused alarm.

During the local elections held in 1958, Soka Gakkai commanded even greater popular notice. In the April 23 election of prefectural assemblymen and city councilmen in the five major cities, fourteen of the twenty-three Soka Gakkai candidates won. In the April 30 elections of other city councils, 185 of 211 Soka Gakkai candidates were elected. In the July 1958, House of Councilors election, Soka Gakkai ran five candidates from the national electorate and one from the Tokyo local, all of whom were successful.

Encouraged by these successes, in January 1962 Soka Gakkai set up the Komei Seiji Remmei (Clean Government League), commonly known as Koseiren. In the House of Councilors election of that year, all nine Koseiren candidates (seven from the national constituency and two from the local) were elected, bringing to fifteen the number of Soka Gakkai members in the upper house of the Diet. Thus Soka Gakkai councilors formed a Komeikai, a group in the upper house with bargaining power.

THE BIRTH OF KOMEITO

On May 3, 1964, at the twenty-seventh general meeting of Soka Gakkai, President Ikeda made a bombshell announcement. Till then, Soka Gakkai had dabbled in politics as one of the Political Department's programs. But from that day, Ikeda said, the Political Department was abolished, and Koseiren would be a full-fledged political party. Thereafter, Soka Gakkai would devote itself to its religious activities while the affiliated political party assumed full command of the political sphere. Furthermore, the new party was to take part in the next general election. At long last, Soka Gakkai was to put up candidates for the House of Representatives.

Observers regarded this announcement as a complete about-face because Soka Gakkai leaders, including both Ikeda and Toda, had always maintained that their political interest was confined to the upper house and local legislatures.

For instance, on May 3, 1961, Ikeda declared:

> The mission of the Political Department is to send many men —men who have ability, high character, and merciful interest in saving people—into the political world. Only when this is done can we see the establishment of a happy society. . . . But we are not a political party. Therefore we will not get into the House of Representatives. We will send out people to the House of Councilors and local legislatures—the areas which have no political color.

Toda had made similar declarations. It seemed that Ikeda had to create a separate, exclusively political body to avoid the charge of self-contradiction. Nevertheless, the real and ultimate objective of Soka Gakkai is *obutsu myogo*, the fusion of government and Buddhism. Toda coined the expression *obutsu myogo* in his treatise *Obutsu Myogo Ron*, serialized in Soka Gakkai's theoretical journal *Daibyakurenge* from August 1956 to April 1957. He derived it from a passage in Nichiren's *Sandai Hihosho* which begins with the statement that the *hommon no kaidan* should be built when "government and Buddhist law are harmoniously blended" *(oho buppo ni myoji buppo oho ni gasshite)*. Therefore Soka Gakkai leaders never had any reason to object to members of their association winning seats in the House of Representatives. Indeed, it seems that all that had prevented them from participating in a general election before was the prospect of failure. Until the organization had sufficient electoral strength, it avoided running candidates in a House of Representatives election.

At the end of 1961, about six months before the July 1962 House of Councilors election, when nine Soka Gakkai candidates were elected, the organization announced that its membership was 2,300,000 households. Since the membership had increased by May 1964 to at least 3,800,000 families, it was claimed, the organization now felt capable of participating in a general election with some success.

After Ikeda's momentous announcement of May 1964, the Clean Government League was reorganized as a political party—Komeito—on November 17, 1964, bringing the number of Japanese political parties to five. In the July 1965 House of Councilors election, the new party ran fourteen candidates: nine from the national constituency, all of the whom were successful, and five from local constituencies, two of whom—from urban areas—were successful. This brought the total of Komeito councilors to twenty. But the real test came with the next general election, held in January 1967. Komeito ran one candidate each from thirty-two constituencies,[1] and twenty-five of them were successful. This made Komeito the third largest opposition party in the House of Representatives—after the Japan Socialist Party and the Japan Democratic Socialist Party—against the Liberal-Democratic Party's majority. Meanwhile, in local legislatures such as the prefectural assemblies and city councils, Komeito membership rose to 2,088 as of June 1969.

---

[1] From three to five seats for the House of Representatives are allocated to a constituency under the Japanese election system.

RATIONALE FOR POLITICAL PARTICIPATION

Fully aware of the criticism that "a religious organization ought not to get into politics," Ikeda on many occasions attempted to justify Soka Gakkai's involvement in politics. On July 12, 1965, at a meeting of the leaders of the Youth Division, he said:

> There are people who say the relationship between Soka Gakkai and Komeito is vague. Let me take this opportunity to make it clear: Soka Gakkai is a religious organization with two different names. Both, believing in Nichiren Daishonin, aim at achieving *obutsu myogo*. This is also true of an individual, who may be a member of Komeito in the area of his political activities but at the same time a member of Soka Gakkai with regard to his faith. He may be a white-collar worker, or he may be a student. Or he may be a doctor. Thus a man's life is one, but it may be viewed in various aspects—political, economic, and cultural. There is no individual who is engaged in political activities alone; nor is there one whose activities are confined to the realm of economics. Conceptually, you may separate the areas of activities, but in reality it is not possible. Likewise, Soka Gakkai and Komeito are one and the same body.

On the same occasion, Ikeda replied to the criticism that Soka Gakkai aimed to establish a theocracy by gaining control of the national legislature and that its *shakubuku* violated the constitutional provision for freedom of worship:

> Let us once again make clear our position of firmly upholding Article 20 of the constitution for freedom of worship. . . . Religious freedom means freedom to believe in a particular religion, freedom to change that faith, and freedom not to believe in any religion. It is also freedom to express one's religious faith to others and to propagate a religion. Therefore this constitutional provision provides for freedom to conduct *shakubuku*, and what else could it do?

Referring to the constitutional provision that "no religious organization shall receive any privilege from the State," Ikeda denied that Soka Gakkai had ever received any privilege from the state or that it would need any in the future. "History eloquently testifies to the fact that a religion that receives special privileges from the state becomes degraded and that such a religion is a powerless religion," Ikeda declared, with obvious allusions to the Buddhism of the Nara period (710–94) and Shinto of more recent history. He said he saw no need to "make our religion the state religion."

On the provision in Article 20 that "no religious organization shall . . . exercise any political authority," which some critics have charged Soka Gakkai with violating, Ikeda commented:

> It is a well-established view that the "political authority" referred to in this article means the right to enact laws, levy taxes, hold trials, and so forth—that is, the rights of governing, possessed by the state and local governments. Therefore let me ask: when has Soka Gakkai exercised any of these rights?

More recently, Ikeda has explained the relationship between Soka Gakkai and Komeito in the following terms. The religious organization is the "soil" from which men and women of ability spring forth to become active in various fields, including politics. In other words, the emergence of a political offshoot of Soka Gakkai is a natural development. Individual Soka Gakkai members who go into politics will naturally try to rectify the government to meet their own religious ideals.

Ikeda finds a parallel in those European political parties that claim to uphold Christian ideals, such as the Christian Democrats of Italy and West Germany. Komeito, he says, is no more the instrument of a religion than these parties are. Politics and religion are strictly separate in the life of a Soka Gakkai politician, he maintains and, as evidence, points to the fact that none of the political pronouncements of Komeito representatives ever refer to religion.

SOKA GAKKAI'S ELECTORAL STRENGTH

It is interesting to compare the figures given for Soka Gakkai membership with the number of votes cast for Komeito candidates in a national election. The following table presents the relevant figures for candidates from the national constituency in the five upper-house (House of Councilors) elections from 1956 to 1968.

Year	Candidates	Seats Won	Votes	Soka Gakkai Membership in Families
1956	4	2	991,552	406,000
1959	5	5	2,486,795	1,177,000
1962	7	7	4,124,269	2,700,000
1965	9	9	5,097,173	5,300,000
1968	9	9	6,656,771	6,600,000

In 1956, the number of votes per Soka Gakkai family was 2.44, whereas in 1965 it had gone down to 0.96. The difference between the two figures—that of the number of votes received by Komeito candidates (including Soka Gakkai-affiliated candidates in pre-1964 years) and that of Soka Gakkai membership—notably narrowed in 1965. Whereas between 1962 and 1965 the membership nearly doubled, the number of votes for Komeito candidates increased by only 23.5 percent.

This may have several explanations. First, the number of member families claimed by Soka Gakkai may bear little relationship to the number of active individual members. In addition, contrary to popular opinion, Soka Gakkai does not control the voting behavior of members. A Soka Gakkai member may vote for a candidate of a party other than Komeito.

Another explanation may be that in recent years the percentage of individual members, rather than family members, in the Soka Gakkai membership may be increasing. Hence the narrowing gap between the family-membership figure and the number of Soka Gakkai votes. In the 1968 election, votes slightly exceeded the claimed membership. Perhaps with such statistics in mind, Ikeda, on May 3, 1966, reduced the official membership figure by half a million to a figure more accurately indicative of active membership.

KOMEITO'S POLICY

Other political parties and individual critics have criticized Komeito for not making its political position clear. They find it difficult to assign Komeito a place in the traditional right-left political spectrum. The question usually asked is whether

Komeito is a "progressive" (meaning leftist) or a "conservative" party. To this, Komeito has replied that it is a party of *chudoshugi* (middle of the road), a synthesis of capitalism and socialism, both of which Komeito rejects as ideologies of the past.

The ideal society Komeito aims to establish is outlined in its official policy declaration:

> Government aims at realizing the happiness of the individual through rectification of the order and systems of society, while Buddhism [Nichiren Shoshu philosophy] attempts to bring true happiness to the individual by removing the causes of unhappiness found in his own life. Therefore it is possible to build a supreme cultural state and an ideal society by merging government and Buddhist philosophy.[2]

This is the principle of *obutsu myogo,* which Komeito upholds as both the key to creating an ideal society and the key to "the realization of world peace." A society founded on the ideal of *obutsu myogo* is a "supreme cultural state," the "third civilization"—that is, it is neither wholly materialistic nor wholly spiritual but a synthesis of both. Such a synthesis is known in Buddhist vocabulary as *shikishin funi:* identification of matter and mind, body and soul. When *obutsu myogo* is applied to the entire world, it will be called the *sekai minzokushugi* (mankind is one) ideal.

In the practical context of Japanese politics, what are the policies and programs that Komeito advocates as steps toward this goal? It has proclaimed itself as a party concerned with the welfare of the masses, and its basic policies may be summarized as follows:

1. Objection to amending the present pacifist constitution. Komeito is opposed to "misimprovement" of the constitution, which it charges the conservative Liberal-Democratic Party with planning.

2. Pacifism. Komeito objects to the manufacture, use, and possession of nuclear weapons, and to experimentation with them, by any power for any reason at all. It proposes the adoption of a resolution, in the name of mankind, that "persons

[2] Komeito Seisakukyoku (Komeito Policy Bureau): *Taishu Fukushi o Mezashite* (Toward the Welfare of the Masses), Komeito, Tokyo, 1966, Vol. 1, p. 32.

responsible for any future use of nuclear weapons in war should be executed." Consequently, Komeito objects to calls at Japanese ports by nuclear-powered submarines and aircraft carriers of the United States or any other foreign power.

3. Foreign policy. Komeito advocates a policy oriented toward the United Nations. It favors the strengthening of economic cooperation among nations and economic and technical assistance to the developing countries. It also advocates "complete neutralism" in foreign relations—that is, no military alliances between Japan and other powers. The Japan-United States Security Treaty must be dissolved by stages during the 1970's, acccrding to Komeito. It also favors increased trade between Japan and Communist China, admission of Communist China to the United Nations, and Japan's recognition of Communist China.

4. National Defense. Komeito argues that Japan's right to self-defense must be recognized. After the dissolution of the Japan-United States Security Treaty, Komeito anticipates the creation of a type of national-guard organization for self-defense. Should a universal collective security system be established by the United Nations, as Komeito hopes, the national guard would become part of the United Nations police force.

5. Domestic policy. Komeito aims to introduce what it calls "welfare economics" in an elaborate program presented in the four volumes of *Fukushi Keizai e no Michi* (The Road to Welfare Economics), totaling 1,138 pages.

Far more important than its policy or election platform, however, is Komeito's role of moral crusader among the other political parties. Komeito Diet members—and local legislature representatives as well—have been active in exposing corruption and irregularities involving members of other parties and administration officials. Their exposés have earned Komeito many a headline in the national press and have at the same time improved the popular image of its parent organization, Soka Gakkai.

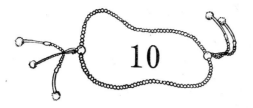

10

Conclusions

WHY SOKA GAKKAI?

The basic factor which permitted the postwar development of Soka Gakkai was the moral hiatus created by Japan's defeat in World War II. After Japan's surrender in August 1945 to the Allied Powers, such presurrender values as State Shinto and emperor worship, and such causes as the Greater East Asia Co-Prosperity Sphere, already negated by defeat, were systematically rooted out by the Allied occupation authorities. This psychological privation, coupled with physical privations, such as shortages of food, shelter, and clothing, killed any sense of national purpose and left individuals with little to strive for beyond personal survival.

Without much success, the Allied Powers endeavored to fill the psychological void with new values such as democracy, the dignity of the individual, and the like. But democracy was merely a political device to the Japanese people, accustomed to an authoritarian government; it did not inspire them as a miraculous cure-all that would solve their immediate problems of hunger, the congestion of living quarters, and so forth. Many turned to the multitude of "new religions"—some of them postwar revivals of prewar cults—for the "instant salvation" they seemed to offer.

Many of these cults have since vanished, except a few that have survived the postwar social changes to claim individual memberships of more than one million.[1] The postwar constitu-

[1] The two largest among the "new religions" are Seicho no Ie, with 1,457,778 members, and PL Kyodan, with 1,265,422, at the end of 1965. (Ministry of Education, *op. cit.*)

tion abolished the state religion and provided for freedom of worship.

Without state support, Shinto all but withered away. Christian conversion made little headway, and during a recent six-year period the number of Japanese Christians increased only by a little over 30,000—from 605,996 at the end of 1959 to 636.123 at the end of 1965.

The appeal of Soka Gakkai in this situation obviously hinged on the fusion of founder Makiguchi's theory of value and Nichiren Shoshu theology, and the dynamic leadership of Makiguchi's number one pupil Josei Toda.

This combination of the doctrine of Nichiren Shoshu and Makiguchi's philosophy appears odd and accidental. Indeed, a critic of Soka Gakkai, a Buddhist scholar, wrote that "no matter how hard I tried, I have been unable to find the reason why Soka Gakkai had to become united with Nichiren Shoshu. The fusion of the two was accidental and not a logical necessity."[2] Of course, Soka Gakkai maintains that Makiguchi's espousal of Nichiren Shoshu was predestined.

Nonetheless, the phenomenal appeal of Soka Gakkai during the first seven years of its postwar history was due as much to the particular nature of the doctrine of Nichiren Shoshu as to Toda's leadership. The doctrine has a number of characteristics. The most important of these is that it developed in Japan many centuries ago. In other words, it is both traditional and indigenous. It is doubtful if a religion, no matter how persuasive its doctrine, could win such a following so rapidly in Japan if it lacked this traditional, national element.

In Toda's lifetime Soka Gakkai's membership grew to 750,000 families. He himself envisioned its reaching the "fantastic" figure of about three million. That membership should soar to over six million in the decade following his death is due primarily to his successor, Ikeda.

Membership increase, however, is not Ikeda's most important contribution to Soka Gakkai. More valuable is his ability to lead the giant organization without signs of schism or dissension. Ikeda's apparently complete authority over Soka

[2] Shinjo Takenaka: *Soka Gakkai*, Rodo Hogaku Shuppan Kabushiki Kaisha, Tokyo, 1967, p. 22.

Gakkai is based on the unswerving allegiance of his followers, which derives from a number of factors. First, Ikeda's understanding of the doctrine is unmatched in the association. His erudition is evident to all in his copious writings and in his addresses. Second, Ikeda seems to be free of the personal failings that have doomed many leaders in history. His highly moral character boosts his prestige among his followers (and in this respect, too, Ikeda differs from his predecessors).

Whether consciously or not, Ikeda strengthens his moral hold over his followers with his humility. When he announces a policy or decision to lower-ranking leaders, Ikeda does not present it as a *fait accompli*. Instead, he says: "We wish to do this. Would you kindly give your consent to this proposal?" Invariably, the response is thunderous applause indicating unconditional approval. Then he says: "Now, let me say that this has been agreed upon unanimously."

With higher-ranking leaders—those with whom he is in closer, day-to-day contact—however, Ikeda is more direct in manner and speech, even to the point of being stern.

When a critic suggested to Ikeda that he was a charismatic leader, Ikeda replied that this was a "fairy tale." He wrote that this critic had concluded that he must be an "absolute leader to members of Soka Gakkai. He makes me blush. Far from it. I am an extremely ordinary young man. . . . I constantly search my soul about my own ignorance, and I am chided and pepped up by members. How is it possible for contemporary men who are full of critical spirit to continue to respect a single human being over a long period of time? Soka Gakkai has no leader who is absolute and supreme. Both the members and myself are comrades, moving forward toward the common objective of *kosen rufu*. This is the reason why I receive the members' support and cooperation—to build the solidarity that gives Soka Gakkai the power to develop."[3]

It cannot be denied that Ikeda has earned the respect and allegiance that he commands with a number of uncommon qualities of the mind. For one, he can address by name every one of the nearly two thousand members of the Board of Directors of Soka Gakkai. When asked to explain his

[3] Daisaku Ikeda: "Answers to Doubts About Komeito," *Jiyu*, IX, May 1967, p. 72.

phenomenal memory, Ikeda replied: "It's because I am so concerned with the welfare of every one of them."

Another quality which is an essential ingredient of Ikeda's personal magnetism is his ability to write—well and profusely. With his tight daily schedule, cluttered with "guidance tours" to local chapters, meetings with visitors, and administrative details, his close aides are puzzled about when he has time to write so much—as, for instance, to produce four volumes of *Ningen Kakumei* in three years.

Soka Gakkai's Future

Now that Soka Gakkai is firmly established in Japanese society and possesses a political potential no one can ignore, what about its future? Will it command an increasingly powerful and important position in Japanese life, or will its strength diminish so that it loses its prominence and is lost in the welter of popular fads?

Any answer to these questions can only be a prediction based on Soka Gakkai's present position. The association is now regarded as, by and large, respectable, and its political party, Komeito, is an asset. The party represents hope for those citizens who have despaired of other political parties of both the right and the left.

One factor favoring Soka Gakkai's survival, if not its spectacular growth, is its flexibility in the interpretation and application of doctrine. It seems to have enabled Ikeda to modify the policies and programs of his predecessors to improve Soka Gakkai's public image.

The flexibility derives from a pair of contrastive precepts in Buddhist theology: *zuien shinnyo no chi* (wisdom to adapt truth to varying circumstances) and *fuhen shinnyo no ri* (the rationality of immutable truth). Thus it may be argued that what appears to be a deviation from the orthodox is an instance of the former while the "immutable truth" remains intact. To put it another way, "absolute truth is immutable, but it assumes varied aspects under varying circumstances."

Such an abstract axiom may be invoked to rationalize an endless variety of policies. If Soka Gakkai moderates its policy of *shakubuku,* it is merely an example of the "wisdom of adapting itself to different circumstances." If Soka Gakkai at one time participated only in elections for the House of Councilors and local legislatures, waiting until it had sufficient electoral strength to participate in a general election, this again is an instance of *zuien shinnyo no chi.* Likewise, the goal of converting the entire nation or the entire world may be modified to one-third of the population of Japan by applying the same Buddhist precept.

Another theological formula used to justify changed policies is the concepts of *naisho* and *geyu,* the inner essence as against the external appearance, or true being and its outward manifestation. Thus it may be argued that any apparent change in Soka Gakkai's activities is merely *geyu,* while its *naisho* remains eternal and immutable.

A similar theological formula of contrasting but complementary concepts is *so* and *betsu*—that is, the general and the particular, the abstract principle and its practical instances. This formula is also used to distinguish a superficial, general argument *(so)* from a deeper, analytical view which grasps the underlying truth *(betsu).* For instance, if Soka Gakkai were criticized for diversifying its activities—in sponsoring musical programs or publishing nonreligious magazines—it could reply that superficially it may appear to be a departure from unswerving pursuit of the faith, but the principle underlying such activities is still basic to Soka Gakkai doctrine.

Flexibility, however, must have limits if it is not to cause a system to distintegrate. Unless the leader of an organization commands the unconditional respect of its members, his flexible interpretation of the fundamental doctrines of the organization might create dissension and lead to splinter groups.

If Ikeda's policy of moderation and compromise is maintained, Soka Gakkai is likely to grow in size and strength, and the nature of the organization will almost certainly alter in response to increasing power. Whether it will be able to retain its high social and political ideals in such circumstances is a test Soka Gakkai may have to face.

But for now, Soka Gakkai under Ikeda's leadership may be described as an asset to Japanese society. It gives its members a definite purpose in life, which most Japanese seem to lack. Ikeda's first concern, he told the author, is that every member of his organization should live "a moral, happy life and become a solid member of society, respected and trusted by his fellow citizens." This transformation of Soka Gakkai members Ikeda calls "human revolution"—that is, "reforming or remaking the individual"—and it seems to be a surer, though slow, means of social reform than restructuring the social system overnight.

Ikeda argues that Soka Gakkai's political activities through Komeito are a "consequence" of the "human revolution" so far attained. A political party made up of Soka Gakkai members is "a flower blooming out of the soil prepared by the propagation of our faith."

Ikeda's conciliatory attitude in recent years is manifested by the remark he made to the author: "We and Christianity have something in common: we are both monotheistic religions. Therefore we can respect each other, not being mutually hostile. We can study each other's doctrine and thus elevate ourselves."

This radical departure from the cry of "We must destroy all the evil religions—all other religions!" may be another instance of "adapting the basic, immutable truth to new circumstances."

Appendices

Chronology

* Because pertinent documents were lost during World War II, Soka Gakkai is unable to establish the exact day on which the inaugural meeting took place in 1937.

179

1941	July 20	Magazine *Kachi Sozo* was inaugurated. Membership of Soka Kyoiku Gakkai was 3,000.
1943	June 20	Makiguchi, Toda, and other leaders were arrested.
1944	Nov. 18	Makiguchi died at Sugamo Detention House in Tokyo.
1945	July 3	Toda was released after two years of detention.
1946	Jan. 1	Toda began lectures on the Lotus Sutra.
1947	Oct. 19	2nd general meeting of Soka Gakkai.
1948	Oct. 17	3rd general meeting.
1949	Oct. 23	4th general meeting.
1950	Nov. 12	5th general meeting.
1951	Apr. 6	Membership was about 3,000 families, organized as 12 chapters.
	Apr. 20	Thrice-monthly *Seikyo Shimbun* was inaugurated.
	May 3	Toda was inaugurated as second president of Soka Gakkai.
	Nov. 4	6th general meeting.
	Dec. 31	Membership was announced as 5,728 families.
1952	Dec. 7	7th general meeting. Membership was announced as 20,000 families.
	Dec. 21	Membership was announced as 22,324 families.
1953	May 3	8th general meeting.
	Sept. 6	*Seikyo Shimbun* became a weekly.
	Nov. 13	Soka Gakkai headquarters was moved from Nishi Kanda to Shinanomachi, Tokyo.
	Nov. 22	9th general meeting.
	Dec. 21	Membership was announced as 70,000 families.
1954	Mar. 30	Daisaku Ikeda was appointed chief of staff.
	May 3	10th general meeting.
	Nov. 3	11th general meeting.
	Nov. 22	Culture Bureau was established.
	Dec. 23	Membership was announced as 164,272 families.
1955	May 3	12th general meeting.
	Nov. 3	13th general meeting.
	Dec. 23	Membership was announced as 194,239 families.
1956	May 3	14th general meeting.
	July 10	Three members were elected to the House of Councilors.
	Nov. 1	15th general meeting.
	Dec. 21	Membership was announced as 500,000 families.
1957	May 3	16th general meeting.
	Nov. 8	17th general meeting.
	Dec. 25	Membership was announced as 750,000 families.
1958	Apr. 2	Josei Toda died.
	Apr. 20	Toda's funeral services were attended by 250,000 members.
	May 3	18th general meeting.
	June 30	Daisaku Ikeda was appointed general director.

	Nov. 9	19th general meeting.
	Dec. 25	Membership was announced as 1,050,000 families.
1959	Apr. 24	261 members were elected to local legislatures.
	May 3	20th general meeting.
	June 3	All six candidates for the House of Councilors were elected.
	Nov. 8	21st general meeting.
	Dec. 2	Nittatsu became 66th-generation high priest at Taiseki-ji.
	Dec. 23	Membership was announced as 1,300,000 families.
1960	Apr. 19	Ikeda became third president of Soka Gakkai.
	Apr. 22	22nd general meeting. Ikeda was formally inaugurated.
	July 29	Membership was announced as 1,500,000 families.
	Dec. 21	Membership was announced as 1,720,000 families.
1961	May 3	23rd general meeting.
	June 27	Membership was announced as 2,000,000 families.
	July 21–24	Daikyakuden fund-raising drive produced total of ¥3,198,824,377.
	Dec. 23	Membership was announced as 2,300,000 families.
1962	Mar. 3	Ikeda was appointed *daikoto* (head of *ko*) of Hokke-ko by Taiseki-ji.
	Apr. 2	Construction of Daikyakuden was started. *Komei Shimbun* was inaugurated.
	May 3	24th general meeting.
	July 1	All nine candidates for the House of Councilors were elected.
	Nov. 27	Membership was announced as 3,000,000 families.
1963	May 3	25th general meeting.
	Sept. 1	26th general meeting. New headquarters building was completed.
	Nov. 30	Membership was announced as 3,950,000 families.
1964	Apr. 1	Completion of Daikyakuden was celebrated. Ikeda was appointed *sokoto* (general head of *ko*) of Hokke-ko.
	May 3	27th general meeting. Participation in general elections, seven-year membership drive target of 6,000,000 families, and plan to build the Shohondo were announced.
	Nov. 17	Komeito was inaugurated.
	Dec.	Membership was announced as 4,310,000 families.
1965	May 3	28th general meeting.
	July 5	Eleven members elected to the House of Councilors.
	Oct. 17	Ikeda presented Nittatsu with an offertory of ¥35,536,004,309 for building the Shohondo.
	Dec.	Membership was announced as 5,500,000 families.
1966	May 3	29th general meeting. Ikeda announced subtraction of 500,000 from aggregate membership figure. Net

		membership was estimated at 5,000,000 families.
	Sept. 25	From this time on, Soka Gakkai was to be called Nichiren Shoshu abroad "to dispel misunderstanding."
	Dec.	Net membership was announced as 6,000,000 families.
1967	Jan. 29	25 out of 32 candidates were elected to House of Representatives.
	May 3	30th general meeting.
	Aug. 7	Student Division membership was announced as 200,000.
	Oct. 12	Invocation ceremony was held for the Shohondo at Taiseki-ji.
	Oct. 15	Tokyo Culture Festival was held at National Stadium, Tokyo.
1968	May 3	31st general meeting. 8th anniversary of Ikeda's assuming presidency. Ikeda announced opening of Soka University in April 1971.
	July 7	Komeito seats in the House of Councilors increased from 20 to 24 as the result of an election in which 13 out of 14 Komeito candidates were successful.
	Sept. 8	At a general meeting of the Student Division, Ikeda urged a Sino-Japanese summit meeting and Japan's recognition of Communist China.

Bibliography

Akiya, Josei, ed.: *Soka Gakkai no Rinen to Jissen* (The Ideals and Practice of Soka Gakkai), Otori Shoin, Tokyo, 1964

Flagler, J. M.: "A Reporter at Large: A Chanting in Japan," *The New Yorker*, November 26, 1966

Hojo, Hiroshi: "Chudoshugi koso Shinjitsu no Kakushin Seito" (Middle of the Road: A True Progressive Party," *Komei*, VI, May 1968

Hosoi, Nittatsu, ed.: *Shinkun Ryodoku Myoho Renge-kyo Narabi ni Kaiketsu* (The Lotus Sutra with Readings in Chinese and Japanese Styles and Two Related Sutras), Soka Gakkai, Tokyo, 1961

Humphreys, Christmas: *Buddhism*, Penguin Books, Inc., Harmondsworth, England, 1951

Ikeda, Daisaku: *Complete Works of Daisaku Ikeda*, Vol. 1, The Seikyo Press, Tokyo, 1968

———: *Guidance Memo*, The Seikyo Press, Tokyo, 1966

———: *Ikeda Kaicho Zenshu* (Complete Works of President Ikeda), Vol. 1 (Essays), Soka Gakkai, Tokyo, 1967

———: "Komeito e no Gimon ni Kotaeru" (Answers to Doubts About Komeito), *Jiyu*, IX, May 1967

———: *Ningen Kakumei* (The Human Revolution), 4 vols., Seikyo Shimbunsha, Tokyo, 1965–67

———: *Ongi Kuden Kogi* (Lectures on Nichiren's Writings), 2 vols., Soka Gakkai, Tokyo, 1965

———: *Rissho Ankoku Ron Kogi* (Lectures on the *Rissho Ankoku Ron*), Soka Gakkai, Tokyo, 1966

———: "Senso to Hinkon wa Nakuseru ka?" (Can War and Poverty Be Eliminated?), *Bungei Shunju*, XLVI, February 1968

———: *Shido Memo* (From President Ikeda's Guidance), Seikyo Shimbun-sha, Tokyo, 1966

———: *Shidoshu* (Answering Questions), Seikyo Shimbun-sha, Tokyo, 1967

Iwamoto, Yutaka: *Bukkyo Nyumon* (An Introduction to Buddhism), Chuo Koron-sha, Tokyo, 1964

———, and Sakamoto, Yukio, eds.: *Hoke-kyo* (The Lotus Sutra), 3 vols., Iwanami Shoten, Tokyo, 1962–67

Kasahara, Kazuo: "Kamakura Shin Bukkyo kara Edo Juzoku Bukkyo e" (From the new Buddhism of Kamakura to the Subordinate Buddhism of Edo). *Daihorin*, XXXV, February 1968
——: *Kakumei no Shukyo: Ikko Ikki to Soka Gakkai* (The Religions of Revolution: The Ikko Uprising and Soka Gakkai), Jimbutsu Orai-sha, Tokyo, 1964
——: *Seiji to Shukyo: Kiro ni Tatsu Soka Gakkai* (Politics and Religion: Soka Gakkai at the Crossroads). Asoka Shuppan-sha, Tokyo, 1965
Kino, Kazuyoshi: *Inochi no Sekai: Hoke-kyo* (The World of Life: The Lotus Sutra), Chikuma Shobo, Tokyo, 1965
Kodaira, Yoshihei: *Soka Gakkai*, Otori Shoin, Tokyo, 1962
Komei Shimbun Henshukyoku (*Komei Shimbun* Editorial Department): *Komeito no Shucho to Jisseki* (Advocacies and Record of Komeito), Tokyo, 1967
Komeito Seisakukyoku (Komeito Policy Bureau): *Taishu Fukushi o Mezashite* (Toward the Welfare of the Masses), Komeito Seisakukyoku, Tokyo, 1966
——: *Fukushi Keizai e no Michi* (The Road to Welfare Economy), 4 vols., Komeito Kikanshikyoku, Tokyo, 1965–67
——: *Komeito no Shucho: Kokkai Ronso no Kiroku* (Advocacies of Komeito: The Record of Diet Debate), 7 vols., Komeito Seisakukyoku, Tokyo, 1967–68
Kubota, Shobun: *Nichiren Shonin Goden* (A Biography of Nichiren Shonin), Daihorinkaku, Tokyo, 1967
Makiguchi, Tsunesaburo: *Kachiron* (Theory of Value), supplemented by Josei Toda, Soka Gakkai, Tokyo, 1953
Miki, Jun: *Shashin Soka Gakkai* (Soka Gakkai in Photographs), Kawade Shobo, Tokyo, 1968
Minato, Kunizo: *Fuji Taiseki-ji*, Kodansha, Tokyo, 1968
"Minshu no Saiten: 1967 Tokyo Bunkasai" (A Festival of the Masses: The 1967 Tokyo Culture Festival), *Shukan Genron*, III, October 25, 1967
Mombusho (Ministry of Education), ed.: *Shukyo Nenkan, 1966* (Almanac of Religions, 1966), Ministry of Education, Tokyo, 1967
Motai, Kyoko: *Nichiren Shu Nyumon* (An Introduction to Nichiren Shu), Kyoiku Shincho-sha, Tokyo, 1968
Murakami, Shigeyoshi: *Soka Gakkai, Komeito*, Aoki Shoten, Tokyo, 1967
Murata, Kiyoaki: "A Battle of Faiths," *Japan Times*, November 2, 1965
——: "Holy Rollers in the Diet," *Japan Times*, July 21, 1956
——: "Komeito in Election," *Japan Times*, July 22, 1965
——: "Komeito in Next Election," *Japan Times*, August 2, 1966
——: "Komeito's Foreign Policy," *Japan Times*, April 1, 1965
——: "New Force in Politics," *Japan Times*, May 21, 1967
——: "The New Objectives," *Japan Times*, September 23, 1965
——: "The New Political Party," *Japan Times*, November 19, 1964
——: "The Next Seven Years," *Japan Times*, May 14, 1964
——: "The Progress of a Faith," *Japan Times*, April 9, 1964
——: "Religion and Government," *Japan Times*, May 28, 1964

———: "Soka Gakkai and the Press," *Japan Times*, June 11, 1964

———: "Soka Gakkai Eases Policy," *Japan Times*, June 21, 1966

———: "Soka Gakkai in 1967," *Japan Times*, January 15, 1967

———: "The Soka Gakkai Today," *Japan Times*, February 13, 1964

———: "The Year-old Party," *Japan Times*, November 23, 1965

———: "Seiji to Shukyo wa Ryoritsu Subeki ka?" (Can Politics and Religion Coexist"), *Keizai Orai*, XVI, August, 1964

Nakaba, Tadakuni: *Nippon no Choryu* (The Current of Japan), Yuki Shobo, Tokyo, 1968

Nakamura, Hajime, ed.: *Shin Bukkyo Jiten* (New Buddhist Dictionary), Seishin Shobo, Tokyo, 1962

Naramoto, Tatsuya, ed.: *Nippon Rekishi Nempyo* (Chronology of Japanese History), Kawade Shobo Shinsha, Tokyo, 1962

Narikawa, Bunga: *Shiri Soshite Okonau* (Know and Then Act), Kyoiku Shincho-sha, Tokyo, 1965

Nishijima, Hisashi: *Komeito*, Sekka-sha, Tokyo, 1968

Ono, Tatsunosuke: *Nichiren*, Yoshikawa Kobunkan, Tokyo, 1958

Oshima, Masamitsu: "Hitomoji no Ningen Kogaku" (Human Engineering in the Flash Card Pattern), *Ushio*, No. 91, January 1968

Sakamoto, Mamoru: "Ikeda Daisaku-shi e no Shitsumonjo" (An Open Letter to Mr. Daisaku Ikeda), *Jiyu*, IX, March 1967

Saki, Akio: "Shinko Shukyo" (New Religions), *Gendai no Esupuri* (The Esprit of Today), II, July 1964

Seikyo Gurafu (The Seikyo Graphic), Nos. 317 (November 7, 1967), 329 (February 6, 1968), 332 (February 27, 1968). 341 (April 30, 1968)

Seikyo Shimbun, Tokyo

Shigyo, Kaishu: *Nichiren Shu Shinko no Shujuso* (Various Aspects of the Nichiren Shu Faith), Kyoiku Shincho-sha Tokyo, 1966

Sokagakkai, The, revised and enlarged edition, The Seikyo Press, Tokyo, 1962

Soka Gakkai Kyogakubu (Study Department, Soka Gakkai): *Bukkyo Tetsugaku Daijiten* (Encyclopedia of Buddhist Philosophy), 4 vols., Soka Gakkai, Tokyo, 1964–68

———: *Nichiren Shoshu Kyogaku Kaisetsu* (Commentaries on Nichiren Shoshu Doctrine), edited under supervision of Daisaku Ikeda, Soka Gakkai, Tokyo, 1963

———: *Sengo Nijunen to Nippon no Shukyo Kakumei* (Twenty Postwar Years and Religious Revolution in Japan), Otori Shoin, Tokyo, 1966

———: *Shakubuku Kyoten* (Shakubuku Manual) 2nd edition, Soka Gakkai, Tokyo, 1967

"Sutando ni Egaku Hitomoji Gomannin no Himitsu" (The Secrets of Flash Card Patterns Formed by 50,000 Persons in the Stands), *Shukan Genron*, III, October 25, 1967

Tada, Shogo: "Kanzen Churitsu o Mezasu" (We Aim at Complete Neutrality), *Komei*, VI, May 1968

Takasaki, Jikido: "Indo Bukkyo no Rekishi" (The History of Indian Buddhism), *Daihorin*, XXXV, February 1968

Takeiri, Yoshikatsu: "Chudoshugi Kakagete Zenshin" (March Under the

Banner of the Middle of the Road), *Komei*, VI, May 1966

Takenaka, Shinjo: *Soka Gakkai*, Rodo Hogaku Shuppan Kabushiki Kaisha, Tokyo, 1967

——: "Soka Gakkai Rikai no Tame no Gimon: Kan'yo e no Teigen" (Doubts for the Purpose of Understanding Soka Gakkai: A Proposal for Tolerance), *Daihorin*, XXXIII, May 1966

Tamura, Yoshiro: "Soka Gakkai wa Migi o Toru ka Hidari o Toru ka," (Will Soko Gakkai Go Right or Left?), *Daihorin*, XXIX, September 1962

——: *Yogensha no Bukkyo: Rissho Ankoku Ron* (The Buddhism of a Prophet: *Rissho Ankoku Ron*), Chikuma Shobo, Tokyo 1967

Thera, Piyadassi: *The Buddha's Ancient Path*, Rider and Company, London, 1964

Toda, Josei: *Hobembon Juryobon Kogi* (Lectures on Hobembon and and Juryobon), Wako-sha, Tokyo, 1958

——: *Lectures on the Sutra: Hoben and Juryo Chapters*, The Seikyo Press, Tokyo, 1967

——: *Nichiren Daishonin Gosho Judaibu Kogi* (Lectures on Ten Principal Works by Nichiren Daishonin), supplemented by Daisaku Ikeda, 5 vols., Soka Gakkai, Tokyo 1964–65

——: *Toda Josei Zenshu* (Complete Works of Josei Toda), Vols. 2 (Speeches) and 3 (Lectures), Wako-sha, Tokyo, 1965 and 1966

Tokyo Daigaku Hoke-kyo Kenkyukai (Tokyo University Lotus Sutra Study Society): *Nichiren Shoshu Soka Gakkai*, 1st and 2nd editions, Sankibo Busshorin, Tokyo, 1962 and 1967

Watanabe, Shoko: *O-kyo no Hanashi* (Stories of Sutras), Iwanami Shoten, Tokyo, 1967

——: "Shin Shakuson Den" (A New Biography of the Buddha), *Daihorin*, XXXII, September 1965

——: "Shokai Shin'yaku Hoke-kyo" (A Comprehensive New Translation of the Lotus Sutra), *Daihorin*, XXXV, February 1968

Yamaguchi, Akira: *Issemmannin no Kokoro o Tsukanda Himitsu: Soka Gakkai no Shinri Senryaku* (The Secret of Seizing the Hearts of Ten Million People: Soka Gakkai's Psychological Strategy), Takagi Shobo, Tokyo, 1967

Yano, Jun'ya: "Nichibei Ampo no Dankaiteki Kaisho no Hoto" (Ways of Phased Dissolution of the Japan–United States Security Treaty), *Komei*, VI, May 1968

Glossary-Index

Amida-kyo (sutra), 88 (n.)

Amida Nyorai (Amidabutsu), *see* Amitabha

Amitabha (Amida Nyorai), 23, 30, 38

Ananda, 25, 44

Anti-Subversive-Activities Law, invocation of 104–5

Art Division, 4

Asahi Shimbun, 90

asamkhya (infinitely large number), 64

Atsuhara, martyrdom at, 39, 41, 69

Avalokitesvara (Kanzeon Bosatsu), 23

Avici, 30

block system, 143

bodhisattva (one who seeks enlightenment), 23, 25, 35, 37, 46

Boken Shonen (magazine), 92, 122

Buddha (Gautama Siddhartha: historical Buddha), 19, 22, 25, 29, 35, 44, 50, 63, 64

Buddha Gaya, 64

Buddha's death date, 19, 34

Burnouf, Emile Louis, 25

cendala, see *sendara*

Ch'angan, 26

Chih-i, 27, 38, 45

chokusen (imperial decree), 61, 131

Christianity, 49, 76, 79, 172, 176

chudoshugi (middle of the road), 169

Clean Government Party, *see* Komeito

constitutional question regarding Komeito, 161–62, 166–67

conversion, see *shakubuku*

cultural activities of Soka Gakkai, 3–15, 18, 146–47

Culture Bureau, 125

Culture Festival, *see* Tokyo Culture Festival

Cunningham, Alexander, 130 (n.)

Daibyakurenge (Soka Gakkai theoretical journal), 24, 92, 112, 165

Daichidoron (exegesis of Mahayana sutras), 130

Daigohonzon (great object of worship), 18, 19, 44, 48, 52, 107, 112, 135, 158

Daihatsu Nehan-gyo (sutra), 61 (n.)

Daijikkyo, *see* Daishikkyo

Daikodo (Grand Lecture Hall), 114, 115

Daikyakuden (Grand Reception Hall), 119, 125, 158

daimoku (sacred phrase embodying title of Lotus Sutra), 51, 52, 89, 157

Daishikkyo (sutra), 32

daisho sotai (second of the five comparisons), 50

danto (parishioner), 71

187

The "weathermark"
identifies this book as having been
planned, designed, and produced by
John Weatherhill, Inc.
7-6-13 Roppongi, Minato-ku, Tokyo 106
Book design and typography by Ronald V. Bell
Layout of photographs by Naoto Kondo
Composition, printing, and binding by
Tosho Printing Co., Ltd., Tokyo
Set in 10-pt. Linotype Century Expanded
with hand-set Century Expanded for display